FREE Study Skills DVD

Dear Customer,

Thank you for your purchase from Mometrix! We consider it an honor and a privilege that you have purchased our product and we want to ensure your satisfaction.

As a way of showing our appreciation and to help us better serve you, we have developed a Study Skills DVD that we would like to give you for <u>FREE</u>. This DVD covers our *best practices* for getting ready for your exam, from how to use our study materials to how to best prepare for the day of the test.

All that we ask is that you email us with feedback that would describe your experience so far with our product. Good, bad, or indifferent, we want to know what you think!

To get your FREE Study Skills DVD, email freedvd@mometrix.com with *FREE STUDY SKILLS DVD* in the subject line and the following information in the body of the email:

- The name of the product you purchased.
- Your product rating on a scale of 1-5, with 5 being the highest rating.
- Your feedback. It can be long, short, or anything in between. We just want to know your impressions and experience so far with our product. (Good feedback might include how our study material met your needs and ways we might be able to make it even better. You could highlight features that you found helpful or features that you think we should add.)
- Your full name and shipping address where you would like us to send your free DVD.

If you have any questions or concerns, please don't hesitate to contact me directly.

Thanks again!

Sincerely,

Jay Willis
Vice President
jay.willis@mometrix.com
1-800-673-8175

SAT

Subject Test Literature 2019 & 2020

SAT Literature Subject Test Secrets Study Guide

Full-Length Practice Test

Step-by-Step Review Video Tutorials

Written and edited by the Mometrix Texas Teacher Certification Test Team

Printed in the United States of America

This paper meets the requirements of ANSI/NISO Z39.48-1992 (Permanence of Paper).

Mometrix offers volume discount pricing to institutions. For more information or a price quote, please contact our sales department at sales@mometrix.com or 888-248-1219.

Mometrix Media LLC is not affiliated with or endorsed by any official testing organization. All organizational and test names are trademarks of their respective owners.

Paperback
ISBN 13: 978-1-5167-1168-0
ISBN 10: 1-5167-1168-8

DEAR FUTURE EXAM SUCCESS STORY

First of all, **THANK YOU** for purchasing Mometrix study materials!

Second, congratulations! You are one of the few determined test-takers who are committed to doing whatever it takes to excel on your exam. **You have come to the right place.** We developed these study materials with one goal in mind: to deliver you the information you need in a format that's concise and easy to use.

In addition to optimizing your guide for the content of the test, we've outlined our recommended steps for breaking down the preparation process into small, attainable goals so you can make sure you stay on track.

We've also analyzed the entire test-taking process, identifying the most common pitfalls and showing how you can overcome them and be ready for any curveball the test throws you.

Standardized testing is one of the biggest obstacles on your road to success, which only increases the importance of doing well in the high-pressure, high-stakes environment of test day. Your results on this test could have a significant impact on your future, and this guide provides the information and practical advice to help you achieve your full potential on test day.

Your success is our success

We would love to hear from you! If you would like to share the story of your exam success or if you have any questions or comments in regard to our products, please contact us at **800-673-8175** or **support@mometrix.com**.

Thanks again for your business and we wish you continued success!

Sincerely,
The Mometrix Test Preparation Team

Need more help? Check out our flashcards at:
http://mometrixflashcards.com/SATII

TABLE OF CONTENTS

Introduction

Thank you for purchasing this resource! You have made the choice to prepare yourself for a test that could have a huge impact on your future, and this guide is designed to help you be fully ready for test day. Obviously, it's important to have a solid understanding of the test material, but you also need to be prepared for the unique environment and stressors of the test, so that you can perform to the best of your abilities.

For this purpose, the first section that appears in this guide is the **Secret Keys**. We've devoted countless hours to meticulously researching what works and what doesn't, and we've boiled down our findings to the five most impactful steps you can take to improve your performance on the test. We start at the beginning with study planning and move through the preparation process, all the way to the testing strategies that will help you get the most out of what you know when you're finally sitting in front of the test.

We recommend that you start preparing for your test as far in advance as possible. However, if you've bought this guide as a last-minute study resource and only have a few days before your test, we recommend that you skip over the first two Secret Keys since they address a long-term study plan.

If you struggle with **test anxiety**, we strongly encourage you to check out our recommendations for how you can overcome it. Test anxiety is a formidable foe, but it can be beaten, and we want to make sure you have the tools you need to defeat it.

Secret Key #1 – Plan Big, Study Small

There's a lot riding on your performance. If you want to ace this test, you're going to need to keep your skills sharp and the material fresh in your mind. You need a plan that lets you review everything you need to know while still fitting in your schedule. We'll break this strategy down into three categories.

Information Organization

Start with the information you already have: the official test outline. From this, you can make a complete list of all the concepts you need to cover before the test. Organize these concepts into groups that can be studied together, and create a list of any related vocabulary you need to learn so you can brush up on any difficult terms. You'll want to keep this vocabulary list handy once you actually start studying since you may need to add to it along the way.

Time Management

Once you have your set of study concepts, decide how to spread them out over the time you have left before the test. Break your study plan into small, clear goals so you have a manageable task for each day and know exactly what you're doing. Then just focus on one small step at a time. When you manage your time this way, you don't need to spend hours at a time studying. Studying a small block of content for a short period each day helps you retain information better and avoid stressing over how much you have left to do. You can relax knowing that you have a plan to cover everything in time. In order for this strategy to be effective though, you have to start studying early and stick to your schedule. Avoid the exhaustion and futility that comes from last-minute cramming!

Study Environment

The environment you study in has a big impact on your learning. Studying in a coffee shop, while probably more enjoyable, is not likely to be as fruitful as studying in a quiet room. It's important to keep distractions to a minimum. You're only planning to study for a short block of time, so make the most of it. Don't pause to check your phone or get up to find a snack. It's also important to **avoid multitasking**. Research has consistently shown that multitasking will make your studying dramatically less effective. Your study area should also be comfortable and well-lit so you don't have the distraction of straining your eyes or sitting on an uncomfortable chair.

The time of day you study is also important. You want to be rested and alert. Don't wait until just before bedtime. Study when you'll be most likely to comprehend and remember. Even better, if you know what time of day your test will be, set that time aside for study. That way your brain will be used to working on that subject at that specific time and you'll have a better chance of recalling information.

Finally, it can be helpful to team up with others who are studying for the same test. Your actual studying should be done in as isolated an environment as possible, but the work of organizing the information and setting up the study plan can be divided up. In between study sessions, you can discuss with your teammates the concepts that you're all studying and quiz each other on the details. Just be sure that your teammates are as serious about the test as you are. If you find that your study time is being replaced with social time, you might need to find a new team.

Secret Key #2 – Make Your Studying Count

You're devoting a lot of time and effort to preparing for this test, so you want to be absolutely certain it will pay off. This means doing more than just reading the content and hoping you can remember it on test day. It's important to make every minute of study count. There are two main areas you can focus on to make your studying count:

Retention

It doesn't matter how much time you study if you can't remember the material. You need to make sure you are retaining the concepts. To check your retention of the information you're learning, try recalling it at later times with minimal prompting. Try carrying around flashcards and glance at one or two from time to time or ask a friend who's also studying for the test to quiz you.

To enhance your retention, look for ways to put the information into practice so that you can apply it rather than simply recalling it. If you're using the information in practical ways, it will be much easier to remember. Similarly, it helps to solidify a concept in your mind if you're not only reading it to yourself but also explaining it to someone else. Ask a friend to let you teach them about a concept you're a little shaky on (or speak aloud to an imaginary audience if necessary). As you try to summarize, define, give examples, and answer your friend's questions, you'll understand the concepts better and they will stay with you longer. Finally, step back for a big picture view and ask yourself how each piece of information fits with the whole subject. When you link the different concepts together and see them working together as a whole, it's easier to remember the individual components.

Finally, practice showing your work on any multi-step problems, even if you're just studying. Writing out each step you take to solve a problem will help solidify the process in your mind, and you'll be more likely to remember it during the test.

Modality

Modality simply refers to the means or method by which you study. Choosing a study modality that fits your own individual learning style is crucial. No two people learn best in exactly the same way, so it's important to know your strengths and use them to your advantage.

For example, if you learn best by visualization, focus on visualizing a concept in your mind and draw an image or a diagram. Try color-coding your notes, illustrating them, or creating symbols that will trigger your mind to recall a learned concept. If you learn best by hearing or discussing information, find a study partner who learns the same way or read aloud to yourself. Think about how to put the information in your own words. Imagine that you are giving a lecture on the topic and record yourself so you can listen to it later.

For any learning style, flashcards can be helpful. Organize the information so you can take advantage of spare moments to review. Underline key words or phrases. Use different colors for different categories. Mnemonic devices (such as creating a short list in which every item starts with the same letter) can also help with retention. Find what works best for you and use it to store the information in your mind most effectively and easily.

Secret Key #3 – Practice the Right Way

Your success on test day depends not only on how many hours you put into preparing, but also on whether you prepared the right way. It's good to check along the way to see if your studying is paying off. One of the most effective ways to do this is by taking practice tests to evaluate your progress. Practice tests are useful because they show exactly where you need to improve. Every time you take a practice test, pay special attention to these three groups of questions:

- The questions you got wrong
- The questions you had to guess on, even if you guessed right
- The questions you found difficult or slow to work through

This will show you exactly what your weak areas are, and where you need to devote more study time. Ask yourself why each of these questions gave you trouble. Was it because you didn't understand the material? Was it because you didn't remember the vocabulary? Do you need more repetitions on this type of question to build speed and confidence? Dig into those questions and figure out how you can strengthen your weak areas as you go back to review the material.

Additionally, many practice tests have a section explaining the answer choices. It can be tempting to read the explanation and think that you now have a good understanding of the concept. However, an explanation likely only covers part of the question's broader context. Even if the explanation makes sense, **go back and investigate** every concept related to the question until you're positive you have a thorough understanding.

As you go along, keep in mind that the practice test is just that: practice. Memorizing these questions and answers will not be very helpful on the actual test because it is unlikely to have any of the same exact questions. If you only know the right answers to the sample questions, you won't be prepared for the real thing. **Study the concepts** until you understand them fully, and then you'll be able to answer any question that shows up on the test.

It's important to wait on the practice tests until you're ready. If you take a test on your first day of study, you may be overwhelmed by the amount of material covered and how much you need to learn. Work up to it gradually.

On test day, you'll need to be prepared for answering questions, managing your time, and using the test-taking strategies you've learned. It's a lot to balance, like a mental marathon that will have a big impact on your future. Like training for a marathon, you'll need to start slowly and work your way up. When test day arrives, you'll be ready.

Start with the strategies you've read in the first two Secret Keys—plan your course and study in the way that works best for you. If you have time, consider using multiple study resources to get different approaches to the same concepts. It can be helpful to see difficult concepts from more than one angle. Then find a good source for practice tests. Many times, the test website will suggest potential study resources or provide sample tests.

Practice Test Strategy

When you're ready to start taking practice tests, follow this strategy:

UNTIMED AND OPEN-BOOK PRACTICE

Take the first test with no time constraints and with your notes and study guide handy. Take your time and focus on applying the strategies you've learned.

TIMED AND OPEN-BOOK PRACTICE

Take the second practice test open-book as well, but set a timer and practice pacing yourself to finish in time.

TIMED AND CLOSED-BOOK PRACTICE

Take any other practice tests as if it were test day. Set a timer and put away your study materials. Sit at a table or desk in a quiet room, imagine yourself at the testing center, and answer questions as quickly and accurately as possible.

Keep repeating timed and closed-book tests on a regular basis until you run out of practice tests or it's time for the actual test. Your mind will be ready for the schedule and stress of test day, and you'll be able to focus on recalling the material you've learned.

Secret Key #4 – Pace Yourself

Once you're fully prepared for the material on the test, your biggest challenge on test day will be managing your time. Just knowing that the clock is ticking can make you panic even if you have plenty of time left. Work on pacing yourself so you can build confidence against the time constraints of the exam. Pacing is a difficult skill to master, especially in a high-pressure environment, so **practice is vital**.

Set time expectations for your pace based on how much time is available. For example, if a section has 60 questions and the time limit is 30 minutes, you know you have to average 30 seconds or less per question in order to answer them all. Although 30 seconds is the hard limit, set 25 seconds per question as your goal, so you reserve extra time to spend on harder questions. When you budget extra time for the harder questions, you no longer have any reason to stress when those questions take longer to answer.

Don't let this time expectation distract you from working through the test at a calm, steady pace, but keep it in mind so you don't spend too much time on any one question. Recognize that taking extra time on one question you don't understand may keep you from answering two that you do understand later in the test. If your time limit for a question is up and you're still not sure of the answer, mark it and move on, and come back to it later if the time and the test format allow. If the testing format doesn't allow you to return to earlier questions, just make an educated guess; then put it out of your mind and move on.

On the easier questions, be careful not to rush. It may seem wise to hurry through them so you have more time for the challenging ones, but it's not worth missing one if you know the concept and just didn't take the time to read the question fully. Work efficiently but make sure you understand the question and have looked at all of the answer choices, since more than one may seem right at first.

Even if you're paying attention to the time, you may find yourself a little behind at some point. You should speed up to get back on track, but do so wisely. Don't panic; just take a few seconds less on each question until you're caught up. Don't guess without thinking, but do look through the answer choices and eliminate any you know are wrong. If you can get down to two choices, it is often worthwhile to guess from those. Once you've chosen an answer, move on and don't dwell on any that you skipped or had to hurry through. If a question was taking too long, chances are it was one of the harder ones, so you weren't as likely to get it right anyway.

On the other hand, if you find yourself getting ahead of schedule, it may be beneficial to slow down a little. The more quickly you work, the more likely you are to make a careless mistake that will affect your score. You've budgeted time for each question, so don't be afraid to spend that time. Practice an efficient but careful pace to get the most out of the time you have.

Secret Key #5 – Have a Plan for Guessing

When you're taking the test, you may find yourself stuck on a question. Some of the answer choices seem better than others, but you don't see the one answer choice that is obviously correct. What do you do?

The scenario described above is very common, yet most test takers have not effectively prepared for it. Developing and practicing a plan for guessing may be one of the single most effective uses of your time as you get ready for the exam.

In developing your plan for guessing, there are three questions to address:

- When should you start the guessing process?
- How should you narrow down the choices?
- Which answer should you choose?

When to Start the Guessing Process

Unless your plan for guessing is to select C every time (which, despite its merits, is not what we recommend), you need to leave yourself enough time to apply your answer elimination strategies. Since you have a limited amount of time for each question, that means that if you're going to give yourself the best shot at guessing correctly, you have to decide quickly whether or not you will guess.

Of course, the best-case scenario is that you don't have to guess at all, so first, see if you can answer the question based on your knowledge of the subject and basic reasoning skills. Focus on the key words in the question and try to jog your memory of related topics. Give yourself a chance to bring the knowledge to mind, but once you realize that you don't have (or you can't access) the knowledge you need to answer the question, it's time to start the guessing process.

It's almost always better to start the guessing process too early than too late. It only takes a few seconds to remember something and answer the question from knowledge. Carefully eliminating wrong answer choices takes longer. Plus, going through the process of eliminating answer choices can actually help jog your memory.

Summary: Start the guessing process as soon as you decide that you can't answer the question based on your knowledge.

7

How to Narrow Down the Choices

The next chapter in this book (**Test-Taking Strategies**) includes a wide range of strategies for how to approach questions and how to look for answer choices to eliminate. You will definitely want to read those carefully, practice them, and figure out which ones work best for you. Here though, we're going to address a mindset rather than a particular strategy.

Your chances of guessing an answer correctly depend on how many options you are choosing from.

How many choices you have	How likely you are to guess correctly
5	20%
4	25%
3	33%
2	50%
1	100%

You can see from this chart just how valuable it is to be able to eliminate incorrect answers and make an educated guess, but there are two things that many test takers do that cause them to miss out on the benefits of guessing:

- Accidentally eliminating the correct answer
- Selecting an answer based on an impression

We'll look at the first one here, and the second one in the next section.

To avoid accidentally eliminating the correct answer, we recommend a thought exercise called **the $5 challenge**. In this challenge, you only eliminate an answer choice from contention if you are willing to bet $5 on it being wrong. Why $5? Five dollars is a small but not insignificant amount of money. It's an amount you could afford to lose but wouldn't want to throw away. And while losing $5 once might not hurt too much, doing it twenty times will set you back $100. In the same way, each small decision you make—eliminating a choice here, guessing on a question there—won't by itself impact your score very much, but when you put them all together, they can make a big difference. By holding each answer choice elimination decision to a higher standard, you can reduce the risk of accidentally eliminating the correct answer.

The $5 challenge can also be applied in a positive sense: If you are willing to bet $5 that an answer choice *is* correct, go ahead and mark it as correct.

Summary: Only eliminate an answer choice if you are willing to bet $5 that it is wrong.

Which Answer to Choose

You're taking the test. You've run into a hard question and decided you'll have to guess. You've eliminated all the answer choices you're willing to bet $5 on. Now you have to pick an answer. Why do we even need to talk about this? Why can't you just pick whichever one you feel like when the time comes?

The answer to these questions is that if you don't come into the test with a plan, you'll rely on your impression to select an answer choice, and if you do that, you risk falling into a trap. The test writers know that everyone who takes their test will be guessing on some of the questions, so they intentionally write wrong answer choices to seem plausible. You still have to pick an answer though, and if the wrong answer choices are designed to look right, how can you ever be sure that you're not falling for their trap? The best solution we've found to this dilemma is to take the decision out of your hands entirely. Here is the process we recommend:

Once you've eliminated any choices that you are confident (willing to bet $5) are wrong, select the first remaining choice as your answer.

Whether you choose to select the first remaining choice, the second, or the last, the important thing is that you use some preselected standard. Using this approach guarantees that you will not be enticed into selecting an answer choice that looks right, because you are not basing your decision on how the answer choices look.

This is not meant to make you question your knowledge. Instead, it is to help you recognize the difference between your knowledge and your impressions. There's a huge difference between thinking an answer is right because of what you know, and thinking an answer is right because it looks or sounds like it should be right.

Summary: To ensure that your selection is appropriately random, make a predetermined selection from among all answer choices you have not eliminated.

Test-Taking Strategies

This section contains a list of test-taking strategies that you may find helpful as you work through the test. By taking what you know and applying logical thought, you can maximize your chances of answering any question correctly!

It is very important to realize that every question is different and every person is different: no single strategy will work on every question, and no single strategy will work for every person. That's why we've included all of them here, so you can try them out and determine which ones work best for different types of questions and which ones work best for you.

Question Strategies

READ CAREFULLY

Read the question and answer choices carefully. Don't miss the question because you misread the terms. You have plenty of time to read each question thoroughly and make sure you understand what is being asked. Yet a happy medium must be attained, so don't waste too much time. You must read carefully, but efficiently.

CONTEXTUAL CLUES

Look for contextual clues. If the question includes a word you are not familiar with, look at the immediate context for some indication of what the word might mean. Contextual clues can often give you all the information you need to decipher the meaning of an unfamiliar word. Even if you can't determine the meaning, you may be able to narrow down the possibilities enough to make a solid guess at the answer to the question.

PREFIXES

If you're having trouble with a word in the question or answer choices, try dissecting it. Take advantage of every clue that the word might include. Prefixes and suffixes can be a huge help. Usually they allow you to determine a basic meaning. Pre- means before, post- means after, pro - is positive, de- is negative. From prefixes and suffixes, you can get an idea of the general meaning of the word and try to put it into context.

HEDGE WORDS

Watch out for critical hedge words, such as *likely, may, can, sometimes, often, almost, mostly, usually, generally, rarely,* and *sometimes.* Question writers insert these hedge phrases to cover every possibility. Often an answer choice will be wrong simply because it leaves no room for exception. Be on guard for answer choices that have definitive words such as *exactly* and *always.*

SWITCHBACK WORDS

Stay alert for *switchbacks.* These are the words and phrases frequently used to alert you to shifts in thought. The most common switchback words are *but, although,* and *however.* Others include *nevertheless, on the other hand, even though, while, in spite of, despite, regardless of.* Switchback words are important to catch because they can change the direction of the question or an answer choice.

FACE VALUE

When in doubt, use common sense. Accept the situation in the problem at face value. Don't read too much into it. These problems will not require you to make wild assumptions. If you have to go beyond creativity and warp time or space in order to have an answer choice fit the question, then you should move on and consider the other answer choices. These are normal problems rooted in reality. The applicable relationship or explanation may not be readily apparent, but it is there for you to figure out. Use your common sense to interpret anything that isn't clear.

Answer Choice Strategies

ANSWER SELECTION

The most thorough way to pick an answer choice is to identify and eliminate wrong answers until only one is left, then confirm it is the correct answer. Sometimes an answer choice may immediately seem right, but be careful. The test writers will usually put more than one reasonable answer choice on each question, so take a second to read all of them and make sure that the other choices are not equally obvious. As long as you have time left, it is better to read every answer choice than to pick the first one that looks right without checking the others.

ANSWER CHOICE FAMILIES

An answer choice family consists of two (in rare cases, three) answer choices that are very similar in construction and cannot all be true at the same time. If you see two answer choices that are direct opposites or parallels, one of them is usually the correct answer. For instance, if one answer choice says that quantity x increases and another either says that quantity x decreases (opposite) or says that quantity y increases (parallel), then those answer choices would fall into the same family. An answer choice that doesn't match the construction of the answer choice family is more likely to be incorrect. Most questions will not have answer choice families, but when they do appear, you should be prepared to recognize them.

ELIMINATE ANSWERS

Eliminate answer choices as soon as you realize they are wrong, but make sure you consider all possibilities. If you are eliminating answer choices and realize that the last one you are left with is also wrong, don't panic. Start over and consider each choice again. There may be something you missed the first time that you will realize on the second pass.

AVOID FACT TRAPS

Don't be distracted by an answer choice that is factually true but doesn't answer the question. You are looking for the choice that answers the question. Stay focused on what the question is asking for so you don't accidentally pick an answer that is true but incorrect. Always go back to the question and make sure the answer choice you've selected actually answers the question and is not merely a true statement.

EXTREME STATEMENTS

In general, you should avoid answers that put forth extreme actions as standard practice or proclaim controversial ideas as established fact. An answer choice that states the "process should be used in certain situations, if..." is much more likely to be correct than one that states the "process should be discontinued completely." The first is a calm rational statement and doesn't even make a definitive, uncompromising stance, using a hedge word *if* to provide wiggle room, whereas the second choice is a radical idea and far more extreme.

BENCHMARK

As you read through the answer choices and you come across one that seems to answer the question well, mentally select that answer choice. This is not your final answer, but it's the one that will help you evaluate the other answer choices. The one that you selected is your benchmark or standard for judging each of the other answer choices. Every other answer choice must be compared to your benchmark. That choice is correct until proven otherwise by another answer choice beating it. If you find a better answer, then that one becomes your new benchmark. Once you've decided that no other choice answers the question as well as your benchmark, you have your final answer.

PREDICT THE ANSWER

Before you even start looking at the answer choices, it is often best to try to predict the answer. When you come up with the answer on your own, it is easier to avoid distractions and traps because you will know exactly what to look for. The right answer choice is unlikely to be word-for-word what you came up with, but it should be a close match. Even if you are confident that you have the right answer, you should still take the time to read each option before moving on.

General Strategies

TOUGH QUESTIONS

If you are stumped on a problem or it appears too hard or too difficult, don't waste time. Move on! Remember though, if you can quickly check for obviously incorrect answer choices, your chances of guessing correctly are greatly improved. Before you completely give up, at least try to knock out a couple of possible answers. Eliminate what you can and then guess at the remaining answer choices before moving on.

CHECK YOUR WORK

Since you will probably not know every term listed and the answer to every question, it is important that you get credit for the ones that you do know. Don't miss any questions through careless mistakes. If at all possible, try to take a second to look back over your answer selection and make sure you've selected the correct answer choice and haven't made a costly careless mistake (such as marking an answer choice that you didn't mean to mark). This quick double check should more than pay for itself in caught mistakes for the time it costs.

PACE YOURSELF

It's easy to be overwhelmed when you're looking at a page full of questions; your mind is confused and full of random thoughts, and the clock is ticking down faster than you would like. Calm down and maintain the pace that you have set for yourself. Especially as you get down to the last few minutes of the test, don't let the small numbers on the clock make you panic. As long as you are on track by monitoring your pace, you are guaranteed to have time for each question.

DON'T RUSH

It is very easy to make errors when you are in a hurry. Maintaining a fast pace in answering questions is pointless if it makes you miss questions that you would have gotten right otherwise. Test writers like to include distracting information and wrong answers that seem right. Taking a little extra time to avoid careless mistakes can make all the difference in your test score. Find a pace that allows you to be confident in the answers that you select.

KEEP MOVING

Panicking will not help you pass the test, so do your best to stay calm and keep moving. Taking deep breaths and going through the answer elimination steps you practiced can help to break through a stress barrier and keep your pace.

Final Notes

The combination of a solid foundation of content knowledge and the confidence that comes from practicing your plan for applying that knowledge is the key to maximizing your performance on test day. As your foundation of content knowledge is built up and strengthened, you'll find that the strategies included in this chapter become more and more effective in helping you quickly sift through the distractions and traps of the test to isolate the correct answer.

Now it's time to move on to the test content chapters of this book, but be sure to keep your goal in mind. As you read, think about how you will be able to apply this information on the test. If you've already seen sample questions for the test and you have an idea of the question format and style, try to come up with questions of your own that you can answer based on what you're reading. This will give you valuable practice applying your knowledge in the same ways you can expect to on test day.

Good luck and good studying!

Literary Elements

CONFLICT

A conflict is a problem to be solved. Literary plots typically include one conflict or more. Characters' attempts to resolve conflicts drive the narrative's forward movement. Conflict resolution is often the protagonist's primary occupation. Physical conflicts like exploring, wars, and escapes tend to make plots most suspenseful and exciting. Emotional, mental, or moral conflicts tend to make stories more personally gratifying or rewarding for many audiences. Conflicts can be external or internal. A major type of internal conflict is some inner personal battle, or "man against himself." Major types of external conflicts include "man against nature," "man against man," and "man against society." Readers can identify conflicts in literary plots by identifying the protagonist and antagonist and asking why they conflict, what events develop the conflict, where the climax occurs, and how they identify with the characters.

> **Review Video: Conflict**
> Visit mometrix.com/academy and enter code: 559550

MOOD AND TONE

Mood is a story's atmosphere, or the feelings the reader gets from reading it. The way authors set the mood in writing is comparable to the way filmmakers use music to set the mood in movies. Instead of music, though, writers judiciously select descriptive words to evoke certain moods. The mood of a work may convey joy, anger, bitterness, hope, gloom, fear, an ominous feeling, or any other emotion the author wants the reader to feel. In addition to vocabulary choices, authors also use figurative expressions, particular sentence structures, and choices of diction that project and reinforce the moods they want to create. Whereas mood is the reader's emotions evoked by reading what is written, tone is the emotions and attitudes of the writer that s/he expresses in the writing. Authors use the same literary techniques to establish tone as they do to establish mood. An author may use a humorous tone, an angry or sad tone, a sentimental or unsentimental tone, or something else entirely.

> **Review Video: Style, Tone, and Mood**
> Visit mometrix.com/academy and enter code: 416961

ANALYSIS OF CHARACTER DEVELOPMENT

To understand the meaning of a story, it is vital to understand the characters as the author describes them. We can look for contradictions in what a character thinks, says, and does. We can notice whether the author's observations about a character differ from what other characters in the story say about that character. A character may be dynamic (changing significantly during the story) or static (remaining the same from beginning to end). Characters may be two-dimensional, not fully developed, or may be well developed with characteristics that stand out vividly. Characters may also symbolize universal properties. Additionally, readers can compare and contrast characters to analyze how they were developed.

> **Review Video: Character Changes**
> Visit mometrix.com/academy and enter code: 408719

15

DIALOGUE

Effectively written dialogue serves at least one but usually several purposes. It advances the story and moves the plot. It develops the characters. It sheds light on the work's theme(s) or meaning(s). It can, often subtly, account for the passage of time not otherwise indicated. It can alter the direction that the plot is taking, typically by introducing some new conflict(s) or changing (an) existing one(s). Dialogue can establish a work's narrative voice and the characters' voices and set the tone of the story or of particular characters. When fictional characters display enlightenment or realization, dialogue can give readers an understanding of what those characters have discovered and how. Dialogue can illuminate the motivations and wishes of the story's characters. By using consistent thoughts and syntax, dialogue can support character development. Skillfully created, it can also represent real-life speech rhythms in written form. Via conflicts and ensuing action, dialogue also provides drama.

In fictional works, effectively written dialogue should not only have the effect of breaking up or interrupting sections of narrative. While dialogue may supply exposition for readers, it must nonetheless be believable. Dialogue should be dynamic, not static, and it should not resemble regular prose. Authors should not use dialogue to write clever similes or metaphors, or to inject their own opinions. Nor should they use dialogue at all when narrative would be better; dialogue should not slow the plot movement. Dialogue must seem natural, which means careful construction of phrases rather than actually duplicating natural speech, which does not necessarily translate well to the written word. Finally, all dialogue must be pertinent to the story rather than just added conversation.

FIRST-PERSON NARRATION

First-person narratives let narrators express inner feelings and thoughts, especially when the narrator is the protagonist as Lemuel Gulliver is in Jonathan Swift's *Gulliver's Travels.* The narrator may be a close friend of the protagonist, like Dr. Watson in Arthur Conan Doyle's *Sherlock Holmes.* Or the narrator can be less involved with the main characters and plot, like Nick Carraway in F. Scott Fitzgerald's *The Great Gatsby.* When a narrator reports others' narratives secondhand or more, s/he is a "frame narrator," like the nameless narrator of Joseph Conrad's *Heart of Darkness* or Mr. Lockwood in Emily Brontë's *Wuthering Heights.* First-person plural is unusual but can be effective, as in Isaac Asimov's *I, Robot;* William Faulkner's *A Rose for Emily;* Maxim Gorky's *Twenty-Six Men and a Girl;* or Jeffrey Eugenides' *The Virgin Suicides.* Author Kurt Vonnegut is the first-person narrator in his semi-autobiographical novel *Timequake.* Also unusual but effective is a first-person omniscient (rather than the more common third-person omniscient) narrator, like Death in Markus Zusak's *The Book Thief* and the ghost in Alice Sebold's *The Lovely Bones.*

SECOND-PERSON NARRATION

While second-person address is very commonplace in popular song lyrics, it is the least used form of narrative voice in literary works. Popular serial books of the 1980s like *Fighting Fantasy* or *Choose Your Own Adventure* employed second-person narratives. In some cases, a narrative combines both second-person and first-person voices, speaking of "you" and "I." This can draw readers into the story, and it can also enable the authors to compare directly "your" and "my" feelings, thoughts, and actions. When the narrator is also a character in the story, as in Edgar Allan Poe's short story "The Tell-Tale Heart" or Jay McInerney's novel *Bright Lights, Big City,* the narrative is better defined as first-person despite its also addressing "you."

THIRD-PERSON NARRATION

Narration in the third person is the most prevalent type, as it allows authors the most flexibility. It is so common that readers simply assume without needing to be informed that the narrator is not a character in, or involved in the story. Third-person singular is used more frequently than third-person plural, though some authors have also effectively used plural. However, both singular and plural are most often included in stories according to which character(s) is/are being described. The third-person narrator may be either objective or subjective, and either omniscient or limited. Objective third-person narration does not include what the characters described are thinking or feeling, while subjective third-person narration does. The third-person omniscient narrator knows everything about all characters, including their thoughts and emotions, and all related places, times, and events, whereas the third-person limited narrator may know everything about a particular character of focus, but is limited to that character; in other words, the narrator cannot speak about anything that character does not know.

ALTERNATING-PERSON NARRATION

Although authors more commonly write stories from one point of view, there are also instances wherein they alternate the narrative voice within the same book. For example, they may sometimes use an omniscient third-person narrator and a more intimate first-person narrator at other times. In J. K. Rowling's series of *Harry Potter* novels, she often writes in a third-person limited narrative, but sometimes changes to narration by characters other than protagonist Harry Potter. George R. R. Martin's series *A Song of Ice and Fire* changes the point of view to coincide with divisions between chapters. The same technique is used by Erin Hunter (a pseudonym for several authors of the *Warriors, Seekers,* and *Survivors* book series). Authors using first-person narrative sometimes switch to third-person to describe significant action scenes, especially those where the narrator was absent or uninvolved, as Barbara Kingsolver does in her novel *The Poisonwood Bible.*

Literary Devices and Analysis

LITERAL AND FIGURATIVE MEANING

When language is used literally, the words mean exactly what they say and nothing more. When language is used figuratively, the words mean something more and/or other than what they say. For example, "The weeping willow tree has long, trailing branches and leaves" is a literal description. But "The weeping willow tree looks as if it is bending over and crying" is a figurative description—specifically, a simile or stated comparison. Another figurative language form is metaphor, or an implied comparison. A good example is the metaphor of a city, state, or city-state as a ship, and its governance as sailing that ship. Ancient Greek lyrical poet Alcaeus is credited with first using this metaphor, and ancient Greek tragedian Aeschylus then used it in *Seven Against Thebes,* and then Plato used it in the *Republic.* Henry Wadsworth Longfellow later famously referred to it in his poem, "O Ship of State" (1850), which has an extended metaphor with numerous nautical references throughout.

FIGURATIVE LANGUAGE

Figurative language extends past the literal meanings of words. It offers readers new insight into the people, things, events, and subjects covered in a work of literature. Figurative language also enables readers to feel they are sharing the authors' experiences. It can stimulate the reader's senses, make comparisons that readers find intriguing or even startling, and enable readers to view the world in different ways. Seven specific types of figurative language include: alliteration, personification, imagery, similes, metaphors, onomatopoeia, and hyperbole.

> **Review Video: Figurative Language**
> Visit mometrix.com/academy and enter code: 584902

ALLITERATION, PERSONIFICATION, AND IMAGERY

Alliteration is using a series of words containing the same sounds—assonance with vowels, and consonance with consonants. Personification is describing a thing or animal as a person. Imagery is description using sensory terms that create mental images for the reader of how people, animals, or things look, sound, feel, taste, and/or smell. Alfred Tennyson's poem "The Eagle" uses all of these types of figurative language: "He clasps the crag with crooked hands." Tennyson used alliteration, repeating /k/ and /kr/ sounds. These hard-sounding consonants reinforce the imagery giving visual and tactile impressions of the eagle.

Tennyson also used personification, describing a bird as "he" and calling its talons "hands." In *Romeo and Juliet*, Shakespeare uses personification to describe the changing of the seasons: "When well-appareled April on the heel / Of limping winter treads...." Here "April" and "winter" are given the human characteristics of walking, dressing, and aging.

> **Review Video: Alliteration**
> Visit mometrix.com/academy and enter code: 462837
>
> **Review Video: Personification**
> Visit mometrix.com/academy and enter code: 260066

SIMILES

Similes are stated comparisons using "like" or "as." Similes can be used to stimulate readers' imaginations and appeal to their senses. By comparing fictional characters to well-known objects or experiences, the reader can better relate to them. William Wordsworth's poem about "Daffodils" begins, "I wandered lonely as a cloud." This simile compares his loneliness to that of a cloud. It is also personification, giving a cloud the human quality loneliness. In his novel *Lord Jim* (1900), Joseph Conrad writes in Chapter 33, "I would have given anything for the power to soothe her frail soul, tormenting itself in its invincible ignorance like a small bird beating about the cruel wires of a cage." Conrad uses the word "like" to compare the girl's soul to a small bird. His description of the bird beating at the cage shows the similar helplessness of the girl's soul to gain freedom.

> **Review Video: Simile**
> Visit mometrix.com/academy and enter code: 642949

METAPHORS AND ONOMATOPOEIA

Metaphor is an implied comparison that does not use "like" or "as" the way a simile does. Henry Wadsworth Longfellow echoes the ancient Greeks in "O Ship of State": the metaphor compares the state and its government to a nautical ship and its sailing. Onomatopoeia uses words imitating the sounds of things they name or describe. For example, in his poem "Come Down, O Maid," Alfred Tennyson writes of "The moan of doves in immemorial elms, / And murmuring of innumerable bees." The word "moan" sounds like some sounds doves make, "murmuring" represents the sounds of bees buzzing.

TED HUGHES' ANIMAL METAPHORS

Hughes frequently used animal metaphors in his poetry. In "The Thought Fox," a model of concise, structured beauty, Hughes characterizes the poet's creative process with succinct, striking imagery of an idea entering his head like a wild fox. Repeating "loneliness" in the first two stanzas emphasizes the poet's lonely work: "Something else is alive / Beside the clock's loneliness." He treats an idea's arrival as separate from himself. Three stanzas detail in vivid images a fox's approach from the outside winter forest at starless midnight —its nose, "Cold, delicately" touching

twigs and leaves; "neat" paw prints in snow; "bold" body; brilliant green eyes; and self-contained, focused progress—"Till, with a sudden sharp hot stink of fox," he metaphorically depicts poetic inspiration as the fox's physical entry into "the dark hole of the head." Hughes ends by summarizing his vision of poet as an interior, passive idea recipient, with the outside world unchanged: "The window is starless still; the clock ticks, / The page is printed."

LITERARY EXAMPLES OF METAPHOR

A metaphor is an implied comparison, i.e. it compares something to something else without using "like", "as", or other comparative words. For example, in "The Tyger" (1794), William Blake writes, "Tyger Tyger, burning bright, / In the forests of the night." Blake compares the tiger to a flame not by saying it is like a fire, but by simply describing it as "burning." Henry Wadsworth Longfellow's poem "O Ship of State" (1850) uses an extended metaphor by referring consistently throughout the entire poem to the state, union, or republic as a seagoing vessel, referring to its keel, mast, sail, rope, anchors, and to its braving waves, rocks, gale, tempest, and "false lights on the shore". Within the extended metaphor, Wordsworth uses a specific metaphor: "the anchors of thy hope!"

> **Review Video: Metaphor**
> Visit mometrix.com/academy and enter code: 133295

HYPERBOLE

Hyperbole is excessive exaggeration used for humor or emphasis rather than for literal meaning. For example, in *To Kill a Mockingbird*, Harper Lee narrated, "People moved slowly then. There was no hurry, for there was nowhere to go, nothing to buy and no money to buy it with, nothing to see outside the boundaries of Maycomb County." This was not literally true; Lee exaggerates the scarcity of these things for emphasis. In "Old Times on the Mississippi," Mark Twain wrote, "I... could have hung my hat on my eyes, they stuck out so far." This is not literal, but makes his description vivid and funny. In his poem "As I Walked Out One Evening", W. H. Auden wrote, "I'll love you, dear, I'll love you / Till China and Africa meet, / And the river jumps over the mountain / And the salmon sing in the street." He used things not literally possible to emphasize the duration of his love.

> **Review Video: Hyperbole and Understatement**
> Visit mometrix.com/academy and enter code: 308470

LITERARY IRONY

In literature, irony demonstrates the opposite of what is said or done. Three types are verbal irony, situational irony, and dramatic irony. Verbal irony uses words opposite to the meaning. Sarcasm may use verbal irony. An everyday example is describing something confusing as "clear as mud." In his 1986 movie *Hannah and Her Sisters*, author/director/actor Woody Allen says to his character's date, "I had a great evening; it was like the Nuremburg Trials." Notice these employ similes. In situational irony, what happens contrasts with what was expected. In dramatic irony, narrative informs audiences of more than its characters know. O. Henry's short story *The Gift of the Magi* uses situational irony: a husband and wife each sacrifice their most prized possession to buy each other a Christmas present. The irony is that she sells her long hair to buy him a watch fob, while he sells his heirloom pocket-watch to buy her the jeweled combs for her hair she had long wanted; in the end, neither of them can use their gifts.

LITERARY TERMINOLOGY

In works of prose such as novels, a group of connected sentences covering one main topic is termed a paragraph. In works of poetry, a group of verses similarly connected is called a stanza. In drama, when early works used verse, these were also divided into stanzas or couplets. Drama evolved to use predominantly prose. Overall, whether prose or verse, the conversation in a play is called dialogue. Large sections of dialogue spoken by one actor are called soliloquies or monologues. Dialogue that informs audiences but is unheard by other characters is called an aside. Novels and plays share certain common elements, such as characters (the people in the story), plot (the action of the story), climax (when action and/or dramatic tension reaches its highest point), and denouement (the resolution following the climax). Sections dividing novels are called chapters, while sections of plays are called acts. Subsections of plays' acts are called scenes. Novel chapters are usually not subdivided, although some novels have larger sections divided into groups of chapters.

POETRY

Unlike prose, which traditionally (except in forms like stream of consciousness) consists of complete sentences connected into paragraphs, poetry is written in verses. These may form complete sentences, clauses, or phrases. Poetry may be written with or without rhyme. It can be metered, following a particular rhythmic pattern such as iambic, dactylic, spondaic, trochaic, or anapestic, or may be without regular meter. The terms iamb and trochee, among others, identify stressed and unstressed syllables in each verse. Meter is also described by the number of beats or stressed syllables per verse: dimeter (2), trimeter (3), tetrameter (4), pentameter (5), and so forth. Using the symbol ᴜ to denote unstressed and / to denote stressed syllables, iambic = ᴜ/; trochaic = /ᴜ; spondaic =//; dactylic =/ᴜᴜ; anapestic =ᴜᴜ/. Rhyme schemes identify which lines rhyme, such as ABAB, ABCA, AABA, and so on. Poetry with neither rhyme nor meter is called free verse. Poems may be in free verse, metered but unrhymed, rhymed but without meter, or using both rhyme and meter. In English, the most common meter is iambic pentameter. Unrhymed iambic pentameter is called blank verse.

LITERARY THEORIES AND CRITICISM AND INTERPRETATION

Literary theory gives a rationale for the literary subject matter of criticism, and also for the process of interpreting literature. For example, Aristotle's *Poetics'* requirement of unity underlies any discussion of unity in Sophocles' *Oedipus Rex.* Postcolonial theory, assuming historical racism and exploitation, informs Nigerian novelist and critic Chinua Achebe's contention that in *Heart of Darkness,* Joseph Conrad does not portray Africans with complete humanity. Gender and feminist theories support critics' interpretation of Edna Pontellier's drowning at the climax of Kate Chopin's novel *The Awakening* (1899) as suicide. Until the 19th century, critics largely believed literature referenced objective reality, holding "a mirror up to nature" as William Shakespeare wrote. Twentieth-century Structuralism and New Historicism were predated and influenced by non-traditional, historicized, cross-cultural comparative interpretations of biblical text in 19th-century German "higher criticism." Literary critic Charles Augustin Saint-Beuve maintained that biography could completely explain literature; contrarily, Marcel Proust demonstrated in narrative that art completely transformed biography. A profound 19th-century influence on literary theory was Friedrich Nietzsche's idea that facts must be interpreted to become facts.

Theme and Plot

LITERARY THEME

When we read parables, their themes are the lessons they aim to teach. When we read fables, the moral of each story is its theme. When we read fictional works, the authors' perspectives regarding life and human behavior are their themes. Unlike in parables and fables, themes in literary fiction are not meant to preach or teach the readers a lesson. Hence themes in fiction are not as explicit as they are in parables or fables. Instead they are implicit, and the reader only infers them. By analyzing the fictional characters through thinking about their actions and behavior, and understanding the setting of the story and reflecting on how its plot develops, the reader comes to infer the main theme(s) of the work. When writers succeed, they communicate with their readers such that common ground is established between author and audience. While a reader's individual experience may differ in its details from the author's written story, both may share universal underlying truths which allow author and audience to connect.

> **Review Video: Theme**
> Visit mometrix.com/academy and enter code: 732074

DETERMINING THEME

In well-crafted literature, theme, structure, and plot are interdependent and inextricable: each element informs and reflects the others. The structure of a work is how it is organized. The theme is the central idea or meaning found in it. The plot is what happens in the story. (Plots can be physical actions or mental processes—e.g., Marcel Proust.) Titles can also inform us of a work's theme. For instance, Edgar Allan Poe's title "The Tell-Tale Heart" informs us of its theme of guilt before we even read about the repeated heartbeat the protagonist begins hearing immediately before and constantly after committing and hiding a murder. Repetitive patterns of events or behaviors also give clues to themes. The same is true of symbols: in F. Scott Fitzgerald's *The Great Gatsby*, for Jay Gatsby the green light at the end of the dock symbolizes Daisy Buchanan and his own dreams for the future. More generally, it symbolizes the American Dream, and narrator Nick Carraway explicitly compares it to early settlers' sight of America rising from the ocean.

THEMATIC DEVELOPMENT

In *The Great Gatsby*, F. Scott Fitzgerald portrayed 1920s America as greedy, cynical, and rife with moral decay. Jay Gatsby's lavish weekly parties symbolize the reckless excesses of the Jazz Age. The growth of bootlegging and organized crime in reaction to Prohibition is symbolized by the character of Meyer Wolfsheim and by Gatsby's own ill-gotten wealth. Fitzgerald symbolized social divisions using geography: the "old money" aristocrats like the Buchanans lived on East Egg, while the "new money" bourgeois like Gatsby lived on West Egg. Fitzgerald also used weather, as many authors have, to reinforce narrative and emotional tones in the novel. Just as in *Romeo and Juliet*, William Shakespeare set the confrontation of Tybalt and Mercutio and its deadly consequences on the hottest summer day under a burning sun, in *The Great Gatsby*, Fitzgerald did the same with Tom Wilson's deadly confrontation with Gatsby. Both works are ostensible love stories carrying socially critical themes about the destructiveness of pointless and misguided behaviors—family feuds in the former, pursuit of money in the latter.

In Victor Hugo's novel *Les Misérables*, the overall metamorphosis of protagonist Jean Valjean from a cynical ex-convict into a noble benefactor demonstrates Hugo's theme of the importance of love and compassion for others. Hugo also reflects this in more specific plot events. For example, Valjean's love for Cosette sustains him through many difficult periods and trying events. Hugo illustrates how love and compassion for others beget the same in them: Bishop Myriel's kindness to Valjean eventually inspires him to become honest. Years later, Valjean, as M. Madeleine, has rescued Fauchelevent from under a fallen carriage, Fauchelevent returns the compassionate act by giving Valjean sanctuary in the convent. M. Myriel's kindness also ultimately enables Valjean to rescue Cosette from the Thénardiers. Receiving Valjean's father-like love enables Cosette to fall in love with and marry Marius. And the love between Cosette and Marius enables the couple to forgive Valjean for his past crimes when they are revealed.

In one of his shortest stories, "The Tell-Tale Heart," Poe used economy of language to emphasize the murderer-narrator's obsessive focus on bare details like the victim's cataract-milky eye, the sound of a heartbeat, and insistence he is sane. The narrator begins by denying he is crazy, even citing his extreme agitation as proof of sanity. Contradiction is then extended: the narrator loves the old man, yet kills him. His motives are irrational—not greed or revenge, but to relieve the victim of his "evil eye." Because "eye" and "I" are homonyms, readers may infer that eye/I symbolizes the old man's identity, contradicting the killer's delusion that he can separate them. The narrator distances himself from the old man by perceiving his eye as separate, and dismembering his dead body. This backfires in another body part when he imagines the victim's heartbeat, which is really his own. Guilty and paranoid, he gives himself away. Poe predated Freud in exploring the paradox of killing those we love and the concept of projecting our own processes onto others.

William Faulkner contrasts the traditions of the antebellum South with the rapid changes of post-Civil War industrialization in his short story "A Rose for Emily." Living inside the isolated world of her house, Emily Grierson denies the reality of modern progress. Contradictorily, she is both a testament to time-honored history and a mysterious, eccentric, unfathomable burden. Faulkner portrays her with deathlike imagery even in life, comparing her to a drowned woman and referring to her skeleton. Emily symbolizes the Old South; as her social status is degraded, so is the antebellum social order. Like Miss Havisham in Charles Dickens' *Great Expectations,* Emily preserves her bridal bedroom, denying change and time's passage. Emily tries to control death through denial, shown in her necrophilia with her father's corpse and her killing of Homer Barron to stop him from leaving her, then also denying his death. Faulkner uses the motif of dust throughout to represent not only the decay of Emily, her house, and Old Southern traditions, but also how her secrets are obscured from others.

The great White Whale in *Moby-Dick* plays various roles to different characters. In Captain Ahab's obsessive, monomaniacal quest to kill it, the whale represents all evil, and Ahab believes it his duty and destiny to rid the world of it. Ishmael attempts through multiple scientific disciplines to understand the whale objectively, but fails—it is hidden underwater and mysterious to humans—reinforcing Melville's theme that humans can never know everything; here the whale represents the unknowable. Melville reverses white's usual connotation of purity in Ishmael's dread of white, associated with crashing waves, polar animals, albinos—all frightening and unnatural. White is often viewed as an absence of color, yet white light is the sum total of all colors in the spectrum. In the same way, white can signify both absence of meaning, and totality of meaning incomprehensible to humans. As a creature of nature, the whale also symbolizes how 19th-century white men's exploitative expansionistic actions were destroying the natural environment.

Because of the old fisherman Santiago's struggle to capture a giant marlin, some people characterize Ernest Hemingway's *The Old Man and the Sea* as telling of man against nature. However, it can more properly be interpreted as telling of man's role as part of nature. Both man and fish are portrayed as brave, proud, and honorable. In Hemingway's world, all creatures, including humans, must either kill or be killed. Santiago reflects, "man can be destroyed but not defeated," following this principle in his life. As heroes are often created through their own deaths, Hemingway seems to believe that while being destroyed is inevitable, destruction enables living beings to transcend it by fighting bravely with honor and dignity. Hemingway echoes Romantic poet John Keats' contention that only immediately before death can we understand beauty as it is about to be destroyed. He also echoes ancient Greek and Roman myths and the Old Testament with the tragic flaw of overweening pride or overreaching. Like Icarus, Prometheus, and Adam and Eve, the old man "went out too far."

UNIVERSAL THEMES

The Old Testament book of Genesis, the Quran, and the Epic of Gilgamesh all contain flood stories. Versions differ somewhat: Genesis describes a worldwide flood, attributing it to God's decision that mankind, his creation, had become incontrovertibly wicked in spirit and must be destroyed for the world to start anew. The Quran describes the flood as regional, caused by Allah after sending Nuh (notice the similarity in name to Noah) as a messenger to his people to cease their evil. The Quran stipulates that Allah only destroys those who deny or ignore messages from his messengers. Marked similarities also exist: in the Gilgamesh poems Utnapishtim, like Noah, is instructed to build a ship to survive the flood. Both men send out birds afterward as tests, and both include doves and a raven, though with different outcomes. Historians and archeologists believe a Middle Eastern tidal wave was a real basis for these stories. However, their universal themes remain the same: the flood was seen as God's way of wiping out humans whose behavior had become ungodly.

THEME OF OVERREACHING

A popular theme throughout literature is the human trait of reaching too far or presuming too much. In Greek mythology, Daedalus constructed wings of feathers and wax that men might fly like birds. He permitted his son Icarus to try them, but cautioned the boy not to fly too close to the sun. The impetuous youth (in what psychologist David Elkind later named adolescence's myth of invincibility) ignored this, flying too close to the sun: the wax melted, the wings disintegrated, and Icarus fell into the sea and perished. In the Old Testament, God warned Adam and Eve not to eat fruit from the tree of knowledge of good and evil. Because they ignored this command, they were banished from Eden's eternal perfection, condemning them to mortality and suffering. The Romans were themselves examples of overreaching in their conquest and assimilation of most of the then-known world and ultimate demise. In Christopher Marlowe's *Dr. Faustus* and Johann Wolfgang von Goethe's *Faust,* the protagonist sells his soul to the Devil for unlimited knowledge and success, ultimately leading to his own tragic end.

STORY VS. DISCOURSE

In terms of plot, "story" is the characters, places, and events originating in the author's mind, while "discourse" is how the author arranges and sequences events—which may be chronological or not. Story is imaginary; discourse is words on the page. Discourse allows story to be told in different ways. One element of plot structure is relating events differently from the order in which they occurred. This is easily done with cause-and-effect; for example, in the sentence, "He died following a long illness," we know the illness preceded the death, but the death precedes the illness in words. In Kate Chopin's short story "The Story of an Hour" (1894), she tells some of the events out of chronological order, which has the effect of amplifying the surprise of the ending for the reader. Another element of plot structure is selection. Chopin omits some details, such as Mr. Mallard's trip home; this allows readers to be as surprised at his arrival as Mrs. Mallard is.

PLOT AND MEANING

Novelist E. M. Forster has made the distinction between story as relating a series of events, such as a king dying and then his queen dying, versus plot as establishing motivations for actions and causes for events, such as a king dying and then his queen dying from grief over his death. Thus plot fulfills the function of helping readers understand cause-and-effect in events and underlying motivations in characters' actions, which in turn helps them understand life. This affects a work's meaning by supporting its ability to explain why things happen, why people do things, and ultimately the meaning of life. Some authors find that while story events convey meaning, they do not tell readers there is any one meaning in life or way of living, but rather are mental experiments with various meanings, enabling readers to explore. Hence stories may not necessarily be

23

constructed to impose one definitive meaning, but rather to find some shape, direction, and meaning within otherwise random events.

CLASSIC ANALYSIS OF PLOT STRUCTURE

In *Poetics,* Aristotle defined plot as "the arrangement of the incidents." He meant not the story, but how it is structured for presentation. In tragedies, Aristotle found results driven by chains of cause-and-effect preferable to those driven by the protagonist's personality/character. He identified "unity of action" as necessary for a plot's wholeness; its events must be internally connected, not episodic or relying on *deus ex machina* or other external intervention. A plot must have a beginning, middle, and end. Gustav Freytag adapted Aristotle's ideas into his Triangle/Pyramid (1863). The beginning, today called the exposition/incentive/inciting moment, emphasizes causes and de-emphasizes effects. Aristotle called the ensuing cause-and-effect *desis,* or tying up, today called complication(s) which occur during the rising action. These culminate in a crisis or climax, Aristotle's *peripateia.* This occurs at the plot's middle, where cause and effect are both emphasized. The falling action, which Aristotle called the *lusis* or unraveling, is today called the dénouement. The resolution comes at the catastrophe/outcome or end, when causes are emphasized and effects de-emphasized.

> **Review Video: Plot Line**
> Visit mometrix.com/academy and enter code: 944011

ANALYSIS OF PLOT STRUCTURES THROUGH RECURRING PATTERNS

Authors of fiction select characters, places, and events from their imaginations and arrange them in ways that will affect their readers. One way to analyze plot structure is to compare and contrast different events in a story. For example, in Kate Chopin's "The Story of an Hour," a very simple but key pattern of repetition is the husband's leaving and then returning. Such patterns fulfill the symmetrical aspect that Aristotle said was required of sound plot structure. In James Baldwin's short story, "Sonny's Blues," the narrator is Sonny's brother. In an encounter with one of Sonny's old friends early in the story, the brother initially disregards his communication. In a subsequent flashback, Baldwin informs us that this was the same way he had treated Sonny. In Nathaniel Hawthorne's "Young Goodman Brown," a pattern is created by the protagonist's recurrent efforts not to go farther into the wood; in Herman Melville's "Bartleby the Scrivener," by Bartleby's repeated refusals; and in William Faulkner's "Barn Burning," by the history of barn-burning episodes.

Structure, Genre, and Organization

MAJOR FORMS OF POETRY

From man's earliest days, he expressed himself with poetry. A large percentage of the surviving literature from ancient times is in epic poetry, utilized by Homer and other Greco-Roman poets. Epic poems typically recount heroic deeds and adventures, using stylized language and combining dramatic and lyrical conventions. Epistolary poems also developed in ancient times: poems that are written and read as letters. In the fourteenth and fifteenth centuries, the ballad became a popular convention. Ballads are often structured with rhyme and meter and focus on subjects such as love, death, and religious topics. From these early conventions, numerous other poetic forms developed, such as elegies, odes, and pastoral poems. Elegies are mourning poems written in three parts: lament, praise of the deceased, and solace for loss. Odes evolved from songs to the typical poem of the Romantic time period, expressing strong feelings and contemplative thoughts. Pastoral poems idealize nature and country living. Poetry can also be used to make short, pithy statements. Epigrams (memorable rhymes with one or two lines) and limericks (two lines of iambic dimeter followed by two lines of iambic dimeter and another of iambic trimeter) are known for humor and wit.

HAIKU

Haiku was originally a Japanese poetry form. In the 13th century, haiku was the opening phrase of renga, a 100-stanza oral poem. By the 16th century, haiku diverged into a separate short poem. When Western writers discovered haiku, the form became popular in English, as well as other languages. A haiku has 17 syllables, traditionally distributed across three lines as 5/7/5, with a pause after the first or second line. Haiku are syllabic and unrhymed. Haiku philosophy and technique are that brevity's compression forces writers to express images concisely, depict a moment in time, and evoke illumination and enlightenment. An example is 17th-century haiku master Matsuo Basho's classic: "An old silent pond... / A frog jumps into the pond, / splash! Silence again." Modern American poet Ezra Pound revealed the influence of haiku in his two-line poem "In a Station of the Metro"—line 1 has 5+7 syllables, line 2 has 7, but it still preserves haiku's philosophy and imagistic technique: "The apparition of these faces in the crowd; / Petals on a wet, black bough."

SONNETS

The sonnet traditionally has 14 lines of iambic pentameter, tightly organized around a theme. The Petrarchan sonnet, named for 14th-century Italian poet Petrarch, has an eight-line stanza, the octave, and a six-line stanza, the sestet. There is a change or turn, known as the volta, between the eighth and ninth verses, setting up the sestet's answer or summary. The rhyme scheme is ABBA/ABBA/CDECDE or CDCDCD. The English or Shakespearean sonnet has three quatrains and one couplet, with the rhyme scheme ABAB/CDCD/EFEF/GG. This format better suits English, which has fewer rhymes than Italian. The final couplet often contrasts sharply with the preceding quatrains, as in Shakespeare's sonnets—for example, Sonnet 130, "My mistress' eyes are nothing like the sun...And yet, by heaven, I think my love as rare / As any she belied with false compare." Variations on the sonnet form include Edmund Spenser's Spenserian sonnet in the 16th century, John Milton's Miltonic sonnet in the 17th century, and sonnet sequences. Sonnet sequences are seen

25

in works such as John Donne's *La Corona* and Elizabeth Barrett Browning's *Sonnets from the Portuguese.*

Prose

MAJOR FORMS

Historical fiction is set in particular historical periods, including prehistoric and mythological. Examples include Walter Scott's *Rob Roy* and *Ivanhoe;* Leo Tolstoy's *War and Peace;* Robert Graves' *I, Claudius;* Mary Renault's *The King Must Die* and *The Bull from the Sea* (an historical novel using Greek mythology); Virginia Woolf's *Orlando* and *Between the Acts;* and John Dos Passos's *U.S.A* trilogy. Picaresque novels recount episodic adventures of a rogue protagonist or *pícaro,* like Miguel de Cervantes' *Don Quixote* or Henry Fielding's *Tom Jones.* Gothic novels originated as a reaction against 18th-century Enlightenment rationalism, featuring horror, mystery, superstition, madness, supernatural elements, and revenge. Early examples include Horace Walpole's *Castle of Otranto,* Matthew Gregory Lewis' *Monk,* Mary Shelley's *Frankenstein,* and Bram Stoker's *Dracula.* In America, Edgar Allan Poe wrote many Gothic works. Contemporary novelist Anne Rice has penned many Gothic novels under the pseudonym A. N. Roquelaure. Psychological novels, originating in 17th-century France, explore characters' motivations. Examples include Abbé Prévost's *Manon Lescaut;* George Eliot's novels; Fyodor Dostoyevsky's *Crime and Punishment;* Tolstoy's *Anna Karenina;* Gustave Flaubert's *Madame Bovary;* and the novels of Henry James, James Joyce, and Vladimir Nabokov.

NOVEL OF MANNERS

Novels of manners are fictional stories that observe, explore, and analyze the social behaviors of a specific time and place. While deep psychological themes are more universal across different historical periods and countries, the manners of a particular society are shorter-lived and more varied; the novel of manners captures these societal details. Novels of manners can also be regarded as symbolically representing, in artistic form, certain established and secure social orders. Characteristics of novels of manners include descriptions of a society with defined behavioral codes; the use of standardized, impersonal formulas in their language; and inhibition of emotional expression, as contrasted with the strong emotions expressed in romantic or sentimental novels. Jane Austen's detailed descriptions of English society and characters struggling with the definitions and restrictions placed on them by society are excellent models of the novel of manners. In the 20th century, Evelyn Waugh's *Handful of Dust* is a novel of social manners, and his *Sword of Honour* trilogy is a novel of military manners. Another 20th-century example is *The Unbearable Bassington* by Saki (the pen name of writer H. H. Munro), focusing on Edwardian society.

WESTERN-WORLD SENTIMENTAL NOVELS

Sentimental love novels originated in the movement of Romanticism. Eighteenth-century examples of novels that depict emotional rather than only physical love include Samuel Richardson's *Pamela* (1740) and Jean-Jacques Rousseau's *Nouvelle Héloïse* (1761). Also in the 18th century, Laurence Sterne's novel *Tristram Shandy* (1760-1767) is an example of a novel with elements of sentimentality. The Victorian era's rejection of emotionalism caused the term "sentimental" to have undesirable connotations. Even non-sentimental novelists such as William Makepeace Thackeray and Charles Dickens incorporated sentimental elements in their writing. A 19th-century author of

genuinely sentimental novels was Mrs. Henry Wood (e.g., *East Lynne,* 1861). In the 20th century, Erich Segal's sentimental novel *Love Story* (1970) was a popular bestseller.

EPISTOLARY NOVELS

Epistolary novels are told in the form of letters written by their characters rather than in narrative form. Samuel Richardson, the best-known author of epistolary novels like *Pamela* (1740) and *Clarissa* (1748), widely influenced early Romantic epistolary novels throughout Europe that freely expressed emotions. Richardson, a printer, published technical manuals on letter-writing for young gentlewomen; his epistolary novels were natural fictional extensions of those nonfictional instructional books. Nineteenth-century English author Wilkie Collins' *The Moonstone* (1868) was a mystery written in epistolary form. By the 20th century, the format of well-composed written letters came to be regarded as artificial and outmoded. A 20th-century evolution of letters was tape-recording transcripts in French playwright Samuel Beckett's drama *Krapp's Last Tape.* Though evoking modern alienation, Beckett still created a sense of fictional characters' direct communication without author intervention as Richardson had.

PASTORAL NOVELS

Pastoral novels lyrically idealize country life as idyllic and utopian, akin to the Garden of Eden. *Daphnis and Chloe,* written by Greek novelist Longus around the second or third century, influenced Elizabethan pastoral romances like Thomas Lodge's *Rosalynde* (1590), which inspired Shakespeare's *As You Like It,* and Philip Sidney's *Arcadia* (1590). Jacques-Henri Bernardin de St. Pierre's French work *Paul et Virginie* (1787) demonstrated the early Romantic view of the innocence and goodness of nature. Though the style lost popularity by the 20th century, pastoral elements can still be seen in novels like *The Rainbow* (1915) and *Lady Chatterley's Lover* (1928), both by D. H. Lawrence. Growing realism transformed pastoral writing into less ideal and more dystopian, distasteful and ironic depictions of country life in George Eliot's and Thomas Hardy's novels. Saul Bellow's novel *Herzog* (1964) may demonstrate how urban ills highlight an alternative pastoral ideal. The pastoral style is commonly thought to be overly idealized and outdated today, as seen in Stella Gibbons' pastoral satire, Cold Comfort Farm (1932).

BILDUNGSROMAN

Bildungsroman is German for "education novel." This term is also used in English to describe "apprenticeship" novels focusing on coming-of-age stories, including youth's struggles and searches for things such as identity, spiritual understanding, or the meaning in life. Johann Wolfgang von Goethe's *Wilhelm Meisters Lehrjahre* (1796) is credited as the origin. Charles Dickens' two novels *David Copperfield* (1850) and *Great Expectations* (1861) also fit this form. H. G. Wells wrote *bildungsromans* about questing for apprenticeships to address modern life's complications in *Joan and Peter* (1918), and from a Utopian perspective in *The Dream* (1924). School *bildungsromans* include Thomas Hughes' *Tom Brown's School Days* (1857) and Alain-Fournier's *Le Grand Meaulnes* (1913). Many Hermann Hesse novels, including *Demian, Steppenwolf, Siddhartha, Magister Ludi,* and *Under the Wheel* are *bildungsromans* about struggling, searching youth. Samuel Butler's *The Way of All Flesh* (1903) and James Joyce's *A Portrait of the Artist as a Young Man* (1916) are two modern examples. Variations include J. D. Salinger's *The Catcher in the Rye* (1951), set both within and beyond school, and William Golding's *Lord of the Flies* (1955), a novel not set in a school but one that is a coming-of-age story nonetheless.

ROMAN À CLEF

Roman à clef, French for "novel with a key," refers to books that require a real-life frame of reference, or key, for full comprehension. In Geoffrey Chaucer's *Canterbury Tales,* the Nun's Priest's Tale contains details that confuse readers unaware of history about the Earl of Bolingbroke's involvement in an assassination plot. Other literary works fitting this form include John Dryden's political satirical poem "Absalom and Achitophel" (1681), Jonathan Swift's satire "A Tale of a Tub" (1704), and George Orwell's political allegory *Animal Farm* (1945), all of which cannot be understood completely without knowing their camouflaged historical contents. *Roman à clefs* disguise truths too dangerous for authors to state directly. Readers must know about the enemies of D. H. Lawrence and Aldous Huxley to appreciate their respective novels: Aaron's Rod (1922) and Point Counter Point (1928). Marcel Proust's *Remembrance of Things Past (À la recherché du temps perdu,* 1871-1922) is informed by his social context. James Joyce's *Finnegans Wake* is an enormous *roman à clef* containing multitudinous personal references.

REALISM

Realism is a literary form with the goal of representing reality as faithfully as possible. Its genesis in Western literature was a reaction against the sentimentality and extreme emotionalism of the works written in the literary movement of Romanticism, which championed feelings and their expression. Realists focused in great detail on immediacy of time and place, on specific actions of their characters, and the justifiable consequences of those actions. Some techniques of realism include writing in the vernacular (conversational language), using specific dialects and placing an emphasis on character rather than plot. Realistic literature often addresses ethical issues. Historically, realistic works have often concentrated on the middle classes of the authors' societies. Realists eschew treatments that are too dramatic or sensationalistic as exaggerations of the reality that they strive to portray as closely as they are able. Influenced by his own bleak past, Fyodor Dostoevsky wrote several novels, such as *Crime and Punishment* (1866) that shunned romantic ideals and sought to portray a stark reality. Henry James was a prominent writer of realism in novels such as *Daisy Miller* (1879). Samuel Clemens (Mark Twain) skillfully represented the language and culture of lower-class Mississippi in his novel *Huckleberry Finn* (1885).

SATIRE

Satire uses sarcasm, irony, and/or humor as social criticism to lampoon human folly. Unlike realism, which intends to depict reality as it exists without exaggeration, satire often involves creating situations or ideas deliberately exaggerating reality to be ridiculous to illuminate flawed behaviors. Ancient Roman satirists included Horace and Juvenal. Alexander Pope's poem "The Rape of the Lock" satirized the values of fashionable members of the 18th-century upper-middle class, which Pope found shallow and trivial. The theft of a lock of hair from a young woman is blown out of proportion: the poem's characters regard it as seriously as they would a rape. Irishman Jonathan Swift satirized British society, politics, and religion in works like "A Tale of a Tub." In "A Modest Proposal," Swift used essay form and mock-serious tone, satirically "proposing" cannibalism of babies and children as a solution to poverty and overpopulation. He satirized petty political disputes in *Gulliver's Travels.*

Drama

EARLY DEVELOPMENT

English drama originally developed from religious ritual. Early Christians established traditions of presenting pageants or mystery plays, traveling on wagons and carts through the streets to depict biblical events. Medieval tradition assigned responsibility for performing specific plays to the different guilds. In Middle English, "mystery" meant both religious ritual/truth, and craft/trade. Historically, mystery plays were to be reproduced exactly the same every time like religious rituals. However, some performers introduced individual interpretations of roles and even improvised. Thus drama was born. Narrative detail and nuanced acting were evident in mystery cycles by the

Middle Ages. As individualized performance evolved, plays on other subjects also developed. Middle English mystery plays extant include the York Cycle, Coventry Cycle, Chester Mystery Plays, N-Town Plays, and Towneley/Wakefield Plays. In recent times, these plays began to draw interest again, and several modern actors such as Dame Judi Dench began their careers with mystery plays.

> **Review Video: Dramas**
> Visit mometrix.com/academy and enter code: 216060

DEFINING CHARACTERISTICS

In the Middle Ages, plays were commonly composed in verse. By the time of the Renaissance, Shakespeare and other dramatists wrote plays that mixed prose, rhymed verse, and blank verse. The traditions of costumes and masks were seen in ancient Greek drama, medieval mystery plays, and Renaissance drama. Conventions like asides, in which actors make comments directly to the audience unheard by other characters, and soliloquies (dramatic monologues) were also common during Shakespeare's Elizabethan dramatic period. Monologues dated back to ancient Greek drama. Elizabethan dialogue tended to use colloquial prose for lower-class characters' speech and stylized verse for upper-class characters. Another Elizabethan convention was the play-within-a-play, as in *Hamlet.* As drama moved toward realism, dialogue became less poetic and more conversational, as in most modern English-language plays. Contemporary drama, both onstage and onscreen, includes a convention of breaking the fourth wall, as actors directly face and address audiences.

COMEDY

Today, most people equate the idea of comedy with something funny, and of tragedy with something sad. However, the ancient Greeks defined these differently. Comedy needed not be humorous or amusing: it needed only a happy ending. The classical definition of comedy, as included in Aristotle's works, is any work that tells the story of a sympathetic main character's rise in fortune. According to Aristotle, protagonists needed not be heroic or exemplary: he described them as not evil or worthless, but as ordinary people—"average to below average" morally. Comic figures who were sympathetic were usually of humble origins, proving their "natural nobility" through their actions as their characters were tested, rather than characters born into nobility—who were often satirized as self-important or pompous.

SHAKESPEAREAN COMEDY

William Shakespeare lived in England from 1564-1616. He was a poet and playwright of the Renaissance period in Western culture. He is generally considered the foremost dramatist in world literature and the greatest author to write in the English language. He wrote many poems, particularly sonnets, of which 154 survive today, and approximately 38 plays. Though his sonnets are greater in number and are very famous, he is best known for his plays, including comedies, tragedies, tragicomedies and historical plays. His play titles include: *All's Well That Ends Well, As You Like It, The Comedy of Errors, Love's Labour's Lost, Measure for Measure, The Merchant of Venice, The Merry Wives of Windsor, A Midsummer Night's Dream, Much Ado About Nothing, The Taming of the Shrew, The Tempest, Twelfth Night, The Two Gentlemen of Verona, The Winter's Tale, King John, Richard II, Henry IV, Henry V, Richard III, Romeo and Juliet, Coriolanus, Titus Andronicus, Julius Caesar, Macbeth, Hamlet, Troilus and Cressida, King Lear, Othello, Antony and Cleopatra,* and *Cymbeline.* Some scholars have suggested that Christopher Marlowe wrote several of Shakespeare's works. While most scholars reject this theory, Shakespeare did pay homage to his contemporary, alluding to several of his characters, themes, or verbiage, as well as borrowing themes from several of his plays: Marlowe's *Jew of Malta* influenced Shakespeare's *Merchant of Venice,* etc.

When Shakespeare was writing, during the Elizabethan period of the Renaissance, Aristotle's version of comedies was popular. While some of Shakespeare's comedies were humorous and others were not, all had happy endings. *A Comedy of Errors* is a farce. Based and expanding on a Classical Roman comedy, it is lighthearted and includes slapstick humor and mistaken identity. *Much Ado About Nothing* is a romantic comedy. It incorporates some more serious themes, including social mores; perceived infidelity; marriage's duality as both trap and ideal; and honor and its loss, public shame, and deception, but also much witty dialogue and a happy ending.

DRAMATIC COMEDY

Three types of dramas classified as comedy include the farce, the romantic comedy, and the satirical comedy.

FARCE

The farce is a zany, goofy type of comedy that includes pratfalls and other forms of slapstick humor. The characters appearing in a farce tend to be ridiculous or fantastical in nature. The plot also tends to contain highly improbable events, featuring complications and twists that continue throughout, and incredible coincidences that could never occur in reality. Mistaken identity, deceptions, and disguises are common devices used in farcical comedies. Shakespeare's play *The Comedy of Errors,* with its cases of accidental mistaken identity and slapstick, is an example of farce. Contemporary examples of farce include the Marx Brothers' movies, the Three Stooges movies and TV episodes, and the *Pink Panther* movie series.

ROMANTIC COMEDY

Romantic comedies are probably the most popular of the types of comedy, in both live theater performances and movies. They include not only humor and a happy ending, but also love. In the typical plot of a romantic comedy, two people well suited to one another are either brought together for the first time, or reconciled after being separated. They are usually both sympathetic characters, and seem destined to be together yet separated by some intervening complication—such as ex-lovers, interfering parents or friends, or differences in social class. The happy ending is achieved through the lovers' overcoming all these obstacles. William Shakespeare's *Much Ado About Nothing;* Walt Disney's version of *Cinderella* (1950); Broadway musical *Guys and Dolls* (1955); and movies *Princess Bride* (1987), directed by Rob Reiner; *Sleepless in Seattle* (1993) and *You've Got Mail* (1998), both directed by Nora Ephron and starring Tom Hanks and Meg Ryan; and *Forget Paris* (1995), co-written, produced, directed by and starring Billy Crystal, are examples of romantic comedies.

SATIRICAL COMEDY AND BLACK COMEDY

Satires generally mock and lampoon human foolishness and vices. Satirical comedies fit the classical definition of comedy by depicting a main character's rise in fortune, but they also fit the definition of satire by making that main character either a fool, morally corrupt, or cynical in attitude. All or most of the other characters in the satirical comedy display similar foibles. These include cuckolded spouses, dupes, and other gullible types; tricksters, con artists, and criminals; hypocrites; fortune seekers; and other deceptive types who prey on the latter, who are their willing and unwitting victims. Some classical examples of satirical comedies include *The Birds* by ancient Greek comedic playwright Aristophanes, and *Volpone* by 17th-century poet and playwright Ben Jonson, who made the comedy of humors popular. When satirical comedy is extended to extremes, it becomes black comedy, wherein the comedic occurrences are grotesque or terrible.

TRAGEDY

The opposite of comedy is tragedy, portraying a hero's fall in fortune. While by classical definitions, tragedies could be sad, Aristotle went further, requiring that they depict suffering and pain to cause "terror and pity" in audiences. Additionally, he decreed that tragic heroes be basically good, admirable, and/or noble, and that their downfalls be through personal action, choice, or error, not by bad luck or accident.

ARISTOTLE'S CRITERIA FOR TRAGEDY

In his *Poetics,* Aristotle defined five critical terms relative to tragedy. (1) *Anagnorisis:* Meaning tragic insight or recognition, this is a moment of realization by a tragic hero(ine) when s/he suddenly understands how s/he has enmeshed himself/herself in a "web of fate." (2) *Hamartia:* This is often called a "tragic flaw," but is better described as a tragic error. *Hamartia* is an archery term meaning a shot missing the bull's eye, used here as a metaphor for a mistake—often a simple one—which results in catastrophe. (3) *Hubris:* While often called "pride," this is actually translated as "violent transgression," and signifies an arrogant overstepping of moral or cultural bounds—the sin of the tragic hero who over-presumes or over-aspires. (4) *Nemesis:* translated as "retribution," this represents the cosmic punishment or payback that the tragic hero ultimately receives for committing hubristic acts. (5) *Peripateia:* Literally "turning," this is a plot reversal consisting of a tragic hero's pivotal action, which changes his/her status from safe to endangered.

HEGEL'S THEORY OF TRAGEDY

Georg Wilhelm Friedrich Hegel (1770-1831) proposed a different theory of tragedy than Aristotle (384-322 BCE), which was also very influential. Whereas Aristotle's criteria involved character and plot, Hegel defined tragedy as a dynamic conflict of opposite forces or rights. For example, if an individual believes in the moral philosophy of the conscientious objector, i.e., that fighting in wars is morally wrong, but is confronted with being drafted into military service, this conflict would fit Hegel's definition of a tragic plot premise. Hegel theorized that a tragedy must involve some circumstance in which two values, or two rights, are fatally at odds with one another and conflict directly. Hegel did not view this as good triumphing over evil, or evil winning out over good, but rather as one good fighting against another good unto death. He saw this conflict of two goods as truly tragic. In ancient Greek playwright Sophocles' tragedy *Antigone,* the main character experiences this tragic conflict between her public duties and her family and religious responsibilities.

REVENGE TRAGEDY

Along with Aristotelian definitions of comedy and tragedy, ancient Greece was the origin of the revenge tragedy. This genre became highly popular in Renaissance England, and is still popular today in contemporary movies. In a revenge tragedy, the protagonist has suffered a serious wrong, such as the assault and murder of a family member. However, the wrongdoer has not been punished. In contemporary plots, this often occurs when some legal technicality has interfered with the miscreant's conviction and sentencing, or when authorities are unable to locate and apprehend the criminal. The protagonist then faces the conflict of suffering this injustice, or exacting his or her own justice by seeking revenge. Greek revenge tragedies include *Agamemnon* and *Medea.* Playwright Thomas Kyd's *The Spanish Tragedy* (1582-1592) is credited with beginning the Elizabethan genre of revenge tragedies. Shakespearean revenge tragedies include *Hamlet* (1599-1602) and *Titus Andronicus* (1588-1593). A Jacobean example is Thomas Middleton's *The Revenger's Tragedy* (1606, 1607).

<u>Hamlet's "Tragic Flaw"</u>

Despite virtually limitless interpretations, one way to view Hamlet's tragic error generally is as indecision: He suffers the classic revenge tragedy's conflict of whether to suffer with his knowledge of his mother's and uncle's assassination of his father, or to exact his own revenge and justice against Claudius, who has assumed the throne after his crime went unknown and unpunished. Hamlet's famous soliloquy, "To be or not to be" reflects this dilemma. Hamlet muses "Whether 'tis nobler in the mind to suffer the slings and arrows of outrageous fortune, / Or to take arms against a sea of troubles, / And by opposing end them?" Hamlet both longs for and fears death, as "the dread of something after death … makes us rather bear those ills we have / Than fly to others that we know not … Thus conscience does make cowards of us all." For most of the play, the protagonist struggles with his responsibility in avenging his father, who was killed by Hamlet's uncle Claudius. So Hamlet's tragic error at first might be considered a lack of action. But he then makes several attempts at revenge, each of which end in worse tragedy, until his efforts are ended by the final tragedy – Hamlet's own murder.

MAKING PREDICTIONS

When we read literature, making predictions about what will happen in the writing reinforces our purpose(s) for reading and prepares us mentally. We can make predictions before we begin reading and during our reading. As we read on, we can test the accuracy of our predictions, revise them in light of additional reading, and confirm or refute our predictions. A reader can make predictions by observing the title and illustrations; noting the structure, characters, and subject; drawing on existing knowledge relative to the subject; and asking "why" and "who" questions. Connecting reading to what we already know enables us to learn new information and construct meaning. For example, before third-graders read a book about Johnny Appleseed, they may start a KWL chart—a list of what they *Know*, what they *Want* to know or learn, and what they have *Learned* after reading. Activating existing background knowledge and thinking about the text before reading improves comprehension.

> **Review Video: <u>Predictions</u>**
> Visit mometrix.com/academy and enter code: 437248

DRAWING INFERENCES

Inferences about literary text are logical conclusions that readers make based on their observations and previous knowledge. By inferring, readers construct meanings from text relevant to them personally. By combining their own schemas or concepts and their background information pertinent to the text with what they read, readers interpret it according to both what the author has conveyed and their own unique perspectives. Authors do not always explicitly spell out every meaning in what they write; many meanings are implicit. Through inference, readers can comprehend implied meanings in the text, and also derive personal significance from it, making the text meaningful and memorable to them. Inference is a natural process in everyday life. When readers infer, they can draw conclusions about what the author is saying, predict what may reasonably follow, amend these predictions as they continue to read, interpret the import of themes, and analyze the characters' feelings and motivations through their actions.

> **Review Video: <u>Identifying Logical Conclusions</u>**
> Visit mometrix.com/academy and enter code: 281653

MAKING CONNECTIONS TO ENHANCE COMPREHENSION

Reading involves thinking. For good comprehension, readers make text-to-self, text-to-text, and text-to-world connections. Making connections helps readers understand text better and predict what might occur next based on what they already know, such as how characters in the story feel or what happened in another text. Text-to-self connections with the reader's life and experiences make literature more personally relevant and meaningful to readers. Readers can make connections before, during, and after reading—including whenever the text reminds them of something similar they have encountered in life or other texts. The genre, setting, characters, plot elements, literary structure and devices, and themes an author uses allow a reader to make connections to other works of literature or to people and events in their own lives. Venn diagrams and other graphic organizers help visualize connections. Readers can also make double-entry notes: key content, ideas, events, words, and quotations on one side, and the connections with these on the other.

SUMMARIZING LITERATURE TO SUPPORT COMPREHENSION

When reading literature, especially demanding works, summarizing helps readers identify important information and organize it in their minds. They can also identify themes, problems, and solutions, and can sequence the story. Readers can summarize before, during, and after they read. They should use their own words, as they do when describing a personal event or giving directions. Previewing a text's organization before reading by examining the book cover, table of contents, and illustrations also aids summarizing. So does making notes of key words and ideas in a graphic organizer while reading. Graphic organizers are another useful method: readers skim the text to determine main ideas and then narrow the list with the aid of the organizer. Unimportant details should be omitted in summaries. Summaries can include description, problem-solution, comparison-contrast, sequence, main ideas, and cause-and-effect.

> **Review Video: Summarizing Text**
> Visit mometrix.com/academy and enter code: 172903

EVALUATION OF SUMMARIES

A summary of a literary passage is a condensation in the reader's own words of the passage's main points. Several guidelines can be used in evaluating a summary. The summary should be complete yet concise. It should be accurate, balanced, fair, neutral, and objective, excluding the reader's own opinions or reactions. It should reflect in similar proportion how much each point summarized was covered in the original passage. Summary writers should include tags of attribution, like "Macaulay argues that" to reference the original author whose ideas are represented in the summary. Summary writers should not overuse quotations: they should only quote central concepts or phrases they cannot precisely convey in words other than those of the original author. Another aspect in evaluating a summary is whether it can stand alone as a coherent, unified composition. In addition, evaluation of a summary should include whether its writer has cited the original source of the passage so that readers can find it.

TEXTUAL EVIDENCE TO ANALYZE LITERATURE

Knowing about the historical background and social context of a literary work, as well as the identity of that work's author, can help to inform the reader about the author's concerns and intended meanings. For example, George Orwell published his novel *1984* in the year 1949, soon after the end of World War II. At that time, following the defeat of the Nazis, the Cold War began between the Western Allied nations and the Eastern Soviet Communists. People were therefore concerned about the conflict between the freedoms afforded by Western democracies versus the oppression represented by Communism. Author Orwell had also previously fought in the Spanish Civil War against a Spanish regime that he and his fellows viewed as oppressive. From this information, readers can infer that Orwell was concerned about oppression by totalitarian governments. This informs *1984*'s story of Winston Smith's rebellion against the oppressive "Big

Brother" government of the fictional dictatorial state of Oceania and his capture, torture, and ultimate conversion by that government.

TEXTUAL EVIDENCE TO EVALUATE PREDICTIONS

Textual evidence to evaluate reader predictions about literature includes specific synopses of the work, paraphrases of the work or parts of it, and direct quotations from it. The best literary analysis shows special insight into a theme, character trait, or change. The best textual evidence is strong, relevant, and accurate. Analysis that is not best, but enough, shows reasonable understanding of theme, character trait, or change; contains supporting textual evidence that is relevant and accurate, if not strong; and shows a specific and clear response. Analysis that partially meets criteria also shows reasonable understanding, but the textual evidence is generalized, incomplete, only partly relevant or accurate, or connected only weakly. Inadequate analysis is vague, too general, or incorrect; it may give irrelevant or incomplete textual evidence, or may simply summarize the plot rather than analyzing the work.

> **Review Video: Textual Evidence for Predictions**
> Visit mometrix.com/academy and enter code: 261070

CARPE DIEM TRADITION IN POETRY

Carpe diem is Latin for "seize the day." A long poetic tradition, it advocates making the most of time because it passes swiftly and life is short. It is found in multiple languages, including Latin, Torquato Tasso's Italian, Pierre de Ronsard's French, and Edmund Spenser's English, and is often used in seduction to argue for indulging in earthly pleasures. Roman poet Horace's Ode 1.11 tells younger woman Leuconoe to enjoy the present, not worrying about inevitable aging. Two Renaissance Metaphysical Poets, Andrew Marvell and Robert Herrick, treated *carpe diem* more as a call to action. In "To His Coy Mistress," Marvell points out that time is fleeting, arguing for love, and concluding that because they cannot stop time, they may as well defy it, getting the most out of the short time they have. In "To the Virgins, to Make Much of Time," Herrick advises young women to take advantage of their good fortune in being young by getting married before they become too old to attract men and have babies.

"To His Coy Mistress" begins, "Had we but world enough, and time, / This coyness, lady, were no crime." Using imagery, Andrew Marvell describes leisure they could enjoy if time were unlimited. Arguing for seduction, he continues famously, "But at my back I always hear/Time's winged chariot hurrying near; / And yonder all before us lie / Deserts of vast eternity." He depicts time as turning beauty to death and decay. Contradictory images in "amorous birds of prey" and "tear our pleasures with rough strife / Through the iron gates of life" overshadow romance with impending death, linking present pleasure with mortality and spiritual values with moral considerations. Marvell's concluding couplet summarizes *carpe diem*: "Thus, though we cannot make our sun / Stand still, yet we will make him run." "To the Virgins, to Make Much of Time" begins with the famous "Gather ye rosebuds while ye may." Rather than seduction to live for the present, Robert Herrick's experienced persona advises young women's future planning: "Old time is still a-flying / And this same flower that smiles today, / Tomorrow will be dying."

COUPLETS AND METER TO ENHANCE MEANING IN POETRY

When a poet uses a couplet—a stanza of two lines, rhymed or unrhymed—it can function as the answer to a question asked earlier in the poem, or the solution to a problem or riddle. Couplets can also enhance the establishment of a poem's mood, or clarify the development of a poem's theme. Another device to enhance thematic development is irony, which also communicates the poet's tone and draws the reader's attention to a point the poet is making. The use of meter gives a poem a rhythmic context, contributes to the poem's flow, makes it more appealing to the reader, can represent natural speech rhythms, and produces specific effects. For example, in "The Song of Hiawatha," Henry Wadsworth Longfellow uses trochaic (/ ∪) tetrameter (four beats per line) to evoke for readers the rhythms of Native American chanting: "*By* the *shores* of *Gitche Gum*ee, / *By* the *shin*ing *Big-Sea-Wat*er / *Stood* the *wig*wam *of* No*kom*is." (Italicized syllables are stressed; non-italicized syllables are unstressed.)

EFFECTS OF FIGURATIVE DEVICES ON MEANING IN POETRY

Through exaggeration, hyperbole communicates the strength of a poet's or persona's feelings and enhances the mood of the poem. Imagery appeals to the reader's senses, creating vivid mental pictures, evoking reader emotions and responses, and helping to develop themes. Irony also aids thematic development by drawing the reader's attention to the poet's point and communicating the poem's tone. Thematic development is additionally supported by the comparisons of metaphors and similes, which emphasize similarities, enhance imagery, and affect readers' perceptions. The use of mood communicates the atmosphere of a poem, can build a sense of tension, and evokes the reader's emotions. Onomatopoeia appeals to the reader's auditory sense and enhances sound imagery even when the poem is visual (read silently) rather than auditory (read aloud). Rhyme connects and unites verses, gives the rhyming words emphasis and makes poems more fluent. Symbolism communicates themes, develops imagery, and evokes readers' emotional and other responses.

POETIC STRUCTURE TO ENHANCE MEANING

The opening stanza of Romantic English poet, artist and printmaker William Blake's famous poem "The Tyger" demonstrates how a poet can create tension by using line length and punctuation independently of one another: "Tyger! Tyger! burning bright / In the forests of the night, / What immortal hand or eye / Could frame thy fearful symmetry?" The first three lines of this stanza are trochaic (/∪), with "masculine" endings—that is, strongly stressed syllables at the ends of each of the lines. But Blake's punctuation contradicts this rhythmic regularity by not providing any divisions between the words "bright" and "In" or between "eye" and "Could." This irregular punctuation foreshadows how Blake disrupts the meter at the end of this first stanza by using a contrasting dactyl (/∪∪), with a "feminine" (unstressed) ending syllable in the last word, "symmetry." Thus Blake uses structural contrasts to heighten the intrigue of his work.

In enjambment, one sentence or clause in a poem does not end at the end of its line or verse, but runs over into the next line or verse. Clause endings coinciding with line endings give readers a feeling of completion, but enjambment influences readers to hurry to the next line to finish and understand the sentence. In his blank-verse epic religious poem "Paradise Lost," John Milton wrote: "Anon out of the earth a fabric huge / Rose like an exhalation, with the sound / Of dulcet symphonies and voices sweet, / Built like a temple, where pilasters round / Were set, and Doric pillars overlaid / With golden architrave." Only the third line is end-stopped. Milton, describing the palace of Pandemonium bursting from Hell up through the ground, reinforced this idea through phrases and clauses bursting through the boundaries of the lines. A caesura is a pause in mid-verse. Milton's commas in the third and fourth lines signal caesuras. They interrupt flow, making the narration jerky to imply that Satan's glorious-seeming palace has a shaky and unsound foundation.

REFLECTION OF CONTENT THROUGH STRUCTURE

Wallace Stevens' short yet profound poem "The Snow Man" is reductionist: the snow man is a figure without human biases or emotions. Stevens begins, "One must have a mind of winter," the criterion for realizing nature and life does not inherently possess subjective qualities; we only invest it with these. Things are not as we see them; they simply are. The entire poem is one long sentence of

35

clauses connected by conjunctions and commas, and modified by relative clauses and phrases. The successive phrases lead readers continually to reconsider as they read. Stevens' construction of the poem mirrors the meaning he conveys. With a mind of winter, the snow man, Stevens concludes, "nothing himself, beholds nothing that is not there, and the nothing that is" (ultimate reductionism).

CONTRAST OF CONTENT AND STRUCTURE

Robert Frost's poem "Stopping by Woods on a Snowy Evening" (1923) is deceptively short and simple, with only four stanzas, each of only four lines, and short and simple words. Reinforcing this is Frost's use of regular rhyme and meter. The rhythm is iambic tetrameter throughout; the rhyme scheme is AABA in the first three stanzas and AAAA in the fourth. In an additional internal subtlety, B ending "here" in the first stanza is rhymed with A endings "queer," "near," and "year" of the second; B ending "lake" in the second is rhymed in A endings "shake", "mistake," and "flake" of the third. The final stanza's AAAA endings reinforce the ultimate darker theme. Though the first three stanzas seem to describe quietly watching snow fill the woods, the last stanza evokes the seductive pull of mysterious death: "The woods are lovely, dark and deep," countered by the obligations of living life: "But I have promises to keep, / And miles to go before I sleep, / And miles to go before I sleep." The last line's repetition strengthens Frost's message that despite death's temptation, life's course must precede it.

REPETITION TO ENHANCE MEANING

A villanelle is a nineteen-line poem composed of five tercets and one quatrain. The defining characteristic is the repetition: two lines appear repeatedly throughout the poem. In Theodore Roethke's "The Waking," the two repeated lines are "I wake to sleep, and take my waking slow," and "I learn by going where I have to go." At first these sound paradoxical, but the meaning is gradually revealed through the poem. The repetition also fits with the theme of cycle: the paradoxes of waking to sleep, learning by going, and thinking by feeling represent a constant cycle through life. They also symbolize abandoning conscious rationalism to embrace spiritual vision. We wake from the vision to "Great Nature," and "take the lively air." "This shaking keeps me steady"—another paradox—juxtaposes and balances fear of mortality with ecstasy in embracing experience. The transcendent vision of all life's interrelationship demonstrates, "What falls away is always. And is near." Readers experience the poem holistically, like music, through Roethke's integration of theme, motion, and sound.

Sylvia Plath's villanelle "Mad Girl's Love Song" narrows the scope from universal to personal but keeps the theme of cycle. The two repeated lines, "I shut my eyes and all the world drops dead" and "(I think I made you up inside my head.)" reflect the existential viewpoint that nothing exists in any absolute reality outside of our own perceptions. In the first stanza, the middle line, "I lift my lids and all is born again," in its recreating the world, bridges between the repeated refrain statements—one of obliterating reality, the other of having constructed her lover's existence. Unlike other villanelles wherein key lines are subtly altered in their repetitions, Plath repeats these exactly each time. This reflects the young woman's love, constant throughout the poem as it neither fades nor progresses.

> **Review Video: Structural Elements of Poetry**
> Visit mometrix.com/academy and enter code: 265216

Informational Texts and Rhetoric

FIGURATIVE VS. LITERAL LANGUAGE, DENOTATION VS. CONNOTATION, AND TECHNICAL LANGUAGE

As in fictional literature, informational text also uses both literal language, which means just what it says, and figurative language, which imparts more than literal meaning. For example, an informational text author might use a simile or direct comparison, such as writing that a racehorse "ran like the wind." Informational text authors also use metaphors or implied comparisons, such as "the cloud of the Great Depression." Similar to literal and figurative, denotation is the literal meaning or dictionary definition of a word whereas connotation is feelings or thoughts associated with a word not included in its literal definition. For example, "politician" and "statesman" have the same denotation, but in context, "politician" may have a negative connotation while "statesman" may have a positive connotation. Teachers can help students understand positive or negative connotations of words depending on their sentence contexts. For example, the word "challenge" has a positive connotation in this sentence: "Although I finished last, I still accomplished the challenge of running the race." Teachers can give students a multiple-choice game wherein they choose whether "challenge" here means (A) easy, (B) hard, (C) fun, or (D) taking work to overcome. The word "difficult" has a negative connotation in this sentence: "I finished last in the race because it was difficult." Students choose whether "difficult" here means (A) easy, (B) hard, (C) fun, or (D) lengthy. Positive and negative connotations for the same word can also be taught. Consider the following sentence: "When the teacher asked Johnny why he was in the restroom so long, he gave a *smart* answer." In this context, "smart" means disrespectful and carries a negative connotation. But in the sentence, "Johnny was *smart* to return to class from the restroom right away," the same word means wise and carries a positive connotation. Technical language is vocabulary related to a specific discipline, activity, or process, such as "itemize" when referring to organizing or "kindling" in fire-building instructions.

> **Review Video: Figurative Language**
> Visit mometrix.com/academy and enter code: 584902
>
> **Review Video: Denotation and Connotation**
> Visit mometrix.com/academy and enter code: 310092

EXPLICIT AND IMPLICIT INFORMATION

When informational text states something explicitly, the reader is told by the author exactly what is meant, which can include the author's interpretation or perspective of events. For example, a professor writes, "I have seen students go into an absolute panic just because they weren't able to finish administering the Peabody [Picture Vocabulary Test] in the time they were allotted." This explicitly tells the reader that the students were afraid, and by using the words "just because," the writer indicates their fear was exaggerated out of proportion relative to what happened. However, another professor writes, "I have had students come to me, their faces drained of all color, saying 'We weren't able to finish the Peabody.'" This is an example of implicit meaning: the second writer did not state explicitly that the students were panicked. Instead, he wrote a description of their faces being "drained of all color." From this description, the reader can infer the students were so frightened that their faces paled.

TECHNICAL LANGUAGE

Technical language, found in scientific texts, is more impersonal than literary and vernacular language. Passive voice tone makes tone impersonal. For example, instead of writing, "We found this a central component of protein metabolism," scientists write, "This was found a central component of protein metabolism." While science professors traditionally instructed students to avoid active voice because it leads to first-person ("I" and "we") usage, science editors today find passive voice dull and weak. Many journal articles combine both. Tone in technical science writing should be detached, concise, and professional. While one writes in the vernacular, "This chemical has to be available for proteins to be digested," professionals write technically, "The presence of this chemical is required for the enzyme to break the covalent bonds of proteins."

MAKING INFERENCES ABOUT INFORMATIONAL TEXT

With informational text, reader comprehension depends not only on recalling important statements and details, but also on reader inferences based on examples and details. Readers add information from the text to what they already know to draw inferences about the text. These inferences help the readers to fill in the information that the text does not explicitly state, enabling them to understand the text better. When reading a nonfictional autobiography or biography, for example, the most appropriate inferences might concern the events in the book, the actions of the subject of the autobiography or biography, and the message the author means to convey. When reading a nonfictional expository (informational) text, the reader would best draw inferences about problems and their solutions, and causes and their effects. When reading a nonfictional persuasive text, the reader will want to infer ideas supporting the author's message and intent.

STANDARDS FOR CITING TEXTUAL EVIDENCE

Reading standards for informational texts expect sixth-graders to cite textual evidence to support their inferences and analyses. Seventh-graders are expected additionally to identify several specific pieces of textual evidence to defend each of their conclusions. Eighth-graders are expected to differentiate strong from weak textual evidence. Ninth- and 10th-graders are expected to be able to cite thorough evidence as well as strong evidence from text. Eleventh- and 12th-graders are expected, in combination with the previous grade-level standards, to determine which things are left unclear in a text. Students must be able to connect text to their background knowledge and make inferences to understand text, judge it critically, draw conclusions about it, and make their own interpretations of it. Therefore, they must be able to organize and differentiate between main ideas and details in a text to make inferences about them. They must also be able to locate evidence in the text.

PAIRED READING STRATEGY TO IDENTIFY MAIN IDEAS AND DETAILS

Students can support one another's comprehension of informational text by working in pairs. Each student silently reads a portion of text. One summarizes the text's main point, and then the other must agree or disagree and explain why until they reach an agreement. Then each person takes a turn at identifying details in the text portion that support the main idea that they have identified. Finally, they repeat each step with their roles reversed. Each pair of students can keep track of the central ideas and supporting details by taking notes in two columns: one for main ideas and the other for the details that support those main ideas.

TEXT CODING

Some experts (cf. Harvey and Daniels, 2009) recommend text coding or text monitoring as an active reading strategy to support student comprehension of informational texts. As they read, students make text code notations on Post-it Notes or in the margins of the text. Teachers should model text coding for students one or two codes at a time until they have demonstrated all eight codes: A check mark means "I know this." An X means "This is not what I expected." An asterisk (*) means "This is important." A question mark means "I have a question about this." Two question marks mean "I am really confused about this." An exclamation point means "I am surprised at this." An L means "I have learned something new from this." And RR means "I need to reread this part."

TWO-COLUMN NOTES

When students read or listen to an informational text, it can help them find and note main ideas and supporting details by using the "two-column notes" strategy. Teachers should first introduce this strategy to students, model it, and have them practice using it. As students use two-column notes, they can better organize textual information, find data in text supporting conclusions, and evaluate whether textual evidence supports author claims. For example, in analyzing Abraham Lincoln's Gettysburg Address, students put in the Main Ideas column, "Our founding fathers created the U.S." Next to it in the Details column, they place "Conceived in liberty" and "Dedicated to all men being created equal." Under Main Ideas: "Now the U.S. is in a Civil War." Under Details: "Testing whether our nation as conceived can survive." Main Ideas: "We are here to dedicate the Gettysburg battlefield." Details: "The dedication is to those who died in the war," "This is their final resting place," and "This is a fitting and proper thing to do."

STRUCTURES OR ORGANIZATIONAL PATTERNS IN INFORMATIONAL TEXTS

Informational text can be descriptive, invoking the five senses and answering the questions what, who, when, where, and why. Another structure of informational text is sequence and order: Chronological texts relate events in the sequence that they occurred, from start to finish, while how-to texts organize information into a series of instructions in the sequence in which the steps should be followed. Comparison-contrast structures of informational text describe various ideas to their readers by pointing out how things or ideas are similar and how they are different. Cause and effect structures of informational text describe events that occurred, and identify the causes or reasons that those events occurred. Problem and solution structures of informational text introduce and describe problems, and then offer one or more solutions for each problem described.

> **Review Video: Organizational Methods to Structure Text**
> Visit mometrix.com/academy and enter code: 606263

Meaning and Voice

ESSAYS

The basic format of an essay can be said to have three major parts: the introduction, the body, and the conclusion. The body is further divided into the writer's main points. Short and simple essays may have three main points, while essays covering broader ranges and going into more depth can have almost any number of main points, depending on length.

An essay's introduction should answer three questions: (1) What is the subject of the essay? If a student writes an essay about a book, the answer would include the title and author of the book and any additional information needed—such as the subject or argument of the book. (2) How does the essay address the subject? To answer this, the writer identifies the essay's organization by briefly summarizing main points and/or evidence supporting them. (3) What will the essay prove? This is the thesis statement, usually the opening paragraph's last sentence, clearly stating the writer's message.

The body elaborates on all the main points related to the thesis and supporting evidence, introducing one main point at a time. Each body paragraph should state the point, explain its meaning, support it with quotations or other evidence, and then explain how this point and the evidence are related to the thesis. The writer should then repeat this procedure in a new paragraph for each additional main point. In addition to relating each point to the thesis, clearly restating the thesis in at least one sentence of each paragraph is also advisable.

The conclusion reiterates the content of the introduction, including the thesis, to review them for the reader. The essay writer may also summarize the highlights of the argument or description contained in the body of the essay, following the same sequence originally used in the body. For example, a conclusion might look like: Point 1 + Point 2 + Point 3 = Thesis, or Point 1 → Point 2 → Point 3 → Thesis Proof. Good organization makes essays easier for writers to compose and provides a guide for readers to follow. Well-organized essays hold attention better, and are more likely to get readers to accept their theses as valid.

> **Review Video: Reading Essays**
> Visit mometrix.com/academy and enter code: 169166

INFORMATIVE/EXPLANATORY VS. ARGUMENTATIVE WRITING

Informative/explanatory writing begins with the basis that something is true or factual, while argumentative writing strives to prove something that may or may not be true or factual. Whereas argument is intended to persuade readers to agree with the author's position, informative/explanatory text merely provides information and insight to readers. Informative/explanatory writing concentrates on informing readers about why or how something is as it is. This includes offering new information, explaining how a process works, and/or developing a concept for readers. In accomplishing these objectives, the writing may emphasize naming and differentiating various things within a category; providing definitions of things; providing details about the parts of something; explaining a particular function or behavior; and giving readers explanations for why a fact, object, event, or process exists or occurs.

NECESSARY SKILLS FOR INFORMATIVE/EXPLANATORY WRITING

For students to write in informative/explanatory mode, they must be able to locate and select pertinent information from primary and secondary sources. They must also combine their own

40

experiences and existing knowledge with this new information they find. They must not only select facts, details, and examples relevant to their topics, but also learn to incorporate this information into their writing. Students need at the same time to develop their skills in various writing techniques, such as comparing and contrasting, making transitions between topics/points, and citing scenarios and anecdotes related to their topics. In teaching explanatory/informative writing, teachers must "read like writers" to use mentor texts to consider author craft and technique. They can find mentor texts in blogs, websites, newspapers, novels, plays, picture books, and many more. Teachers should know the grade-level writing standards for informative/explanatory writing to select classroom-specific, appropriate mentor texts.

> **Review Video: Informative Text**
> Visit mometrix.com/academy and enter code: 924964

NARRATIVE WRITING

Put simply, narrative writing tells a story. The most common examples of literary narratives are novels. Non-fictional biographies, autobiographies, memoirs, and histories also use narrative. Narratives should tell stories in such a way that the readers learn something, or gain insight or understanding. Students can write more interesting narratives by relating events or experiences that were meaningful to them. Narratives should not begin with long descriptions or introductions, but start with the actions or events. Students should ensure that there is a point to each story by describing what they learned from the experience they narrate. To write effective description, students should include sensory details, asking themselves what they saw, heard, felt/touched, smelled, and tasted during the experiences they describe. In narrative writing, the details should be concrete rather than abstract. Using concrete details enables readers to imagine everything that the writer describes.

> **Review Video: Narratives**
> Visit mometrix.com/academy and enter code: 280100

SENSORY DETAILS AND CONCRETE VS. ABSTRACT DESCRIPTIONS IN NARRATIVE

Students need vivid description to write descriptive essays. Narratives should also include description of characters, things, and events. Students should remember to describe not only the visual detail of what someone or something looks like, but details from other senses as well. For example, they can contrast the feelings of a sea breeze versus a mountain breeze, describe how they think something inedible would taste, and sounds they hear in the same location at different times of day and night. Readers have trouble visualizing images or imagining sensory impressions and feelings from abstract descriptions, so concrete descriptions make these more real.

Concrete language provides information that readers can grasp and may empathize with, while abstract language, which is more general, can leave readers feeling disconnected, empty, or even confused. "It was a lovely day" is abstract, but "The sun shone brightly, the sky was blue, the air felt warm, and a gentle breeze wafted across my skin" is concrete. "Ms. Couch was a good teacher" uses abstract language, giving only a general idea of the writer's opinion. But "Ms. Couch is excellent at helping us take our ideas and turn them into good essays and stories" uses concrete language, giving more specific examples of what makes Ms. Couch a good teacher. "I like writing poems but not essays" gives readers a general idea that the student prefers one genre over another, but not why. But by saying, "I like writing short poems with rhythm and rhyme, but I hate writing five-page essays that go on and on about the same ideas," readers understand that the student prefers the brevity, rhyme, and meter of short poetry over the length and redundancy of longer prose.

41

JOURNALS AND DIARIES

A journal is a personal account of events, experiences, feelings, and thoughts. Many people write journals to confide their feelings and thoughts or to help them process experiences they have had. Since journals are private documents not meant for sharing with others, writers may not be concerned with grammar, spelling, or other mechanics. However, authors may write journals that they expect or hope to publish someday; in this case, they not only express their thoughts and feelings and process their experiences, but they additionally attend to their craft in writing them. Some authors compose journals to document particular time periods or series of related events, such as a cancer diagnosis, treatment, surviving the disease, and how these experiences have changed/affected them; experiences in recovering from addiction; journeys of spiritual exploration and discovery; trips to or time spent in another country; or anything else someone wants to personally document. Journaling can also be therapeutic: some people use them to work through feelings of grief over loss or to wrestle with big decisions.

The Diary of a Young Girl by Dutch Jew Anne Frank (1947) contains her life-affirming, nonfictional diary entries from 1942-1944 while her family hid in an attic from World War II's genocidal Nazis. *Go Ask Alice* (1971) by Beatrice Sparks is a cautionary, fictional novel in the form of diary entries by an unhappy, rebellious teen who takes LSD, runs away from home and lives with hippies, and eventually returns home. Frank's writing reveals an intelligent, sensitive, insightful girl, raised by intellectual European parents—a girl who believes in the goodness of human nature despite surrounding atrocities. Character Alice, influenced by early 1970s counterculture, becomes less optimistic. However, similarities can be found: Frank dies in a Nazi concentration camp while the fictitious Alice dies in a drug overdose; both are unable to escape their surroundings. Additionally, adolescent searches for personal identity are evident in both books.

LETTERS

Letters are messages written to other people. In addition to letters written between individuals, some writers compose letters to the editors of newspapers, magazines, and other publications; some write "Open Letters" to be published and read by the general public. Open letters, while intended for everyone to read, may also identify a group of people or a single person whom the letter directly addresses. In everyday use, the most-used forms are business letters and personal or friendly letters. Both kinds share common elements: business or personal letterhead stationery; the writer's return address at the top; the addressee's address next; a salutation, such as "Dear [name]" or some similar opening greeting, followed by a colon in business letters or a comma in personal letters; the body of the letter, with paragraphs as indicated; and a closing, like "Sincerely/Cordially/Best regards/etc." or "Love," in intimate personal letters.

The Greek word for "letter" is *epistolē*, which became the English word "epistle." The earliest letters were called epistles, including the New Testament's Epistles from the Apostles to the Christians. In ancient Egypt, the writing curriculum in scribal schools included the epistolary genre. Epistolary novels frame a story in the form of letters. For example, 18th-century English novelist Samuel Richardson wrote the popular epistolary novels *Pamela* (1740) and *Clarissa* (1749). Henry Fielding's satire of *Pamela,* entitled *Shamela* (1741) mocked epistolary writing. French author Montesquieu wrote *Lettres persanes* (1721); Jean-Jacques Rousseau wrote *Julie, ou la nouvelle Héloïse* (1761); and Pierre Choderlos de Laclos penned *Les Liaisons dangereuses* (1782), which was adapted into a screenplay for the multiple Oscar-winning 1988 English-language movie *Dangerous Liaisons.* German author Johann Wolfgang von Goethe wrote *The Sorrows of Young Werther* in epistolary form. Frances Brooke also wrote the first North American novel, *The History of Emily Montague* (1769) using epistolary form. In the 19th century, epistolary novels included Honoré de Balzac's *Letters of Two Brides* (1842) and Mary Shelley's *Frankenstein* (1818).

BLOGS

The word "blog" is derived from "web log" and refers to writing done exclusively on the Internet. Readers of reputable newspapers expect quality content and layouts that enable easy reading. These expectations also apply to blogs. For example, readers can easily move visually from line to line when columns are narrow; overly wide columns cause readers to lose their places. Blogs must also be posted with layouts enabling online readers to follow them easily. However, because the way people read on computer, tablet, and smartphone screens differs from how they read print on paper, formatting and writing blog content is more complex than writing newspaper articles. Two major principles are the bases for blog-writing rules: (1) While readers of print articles skim to estimate their length, online they must scroll down to scan; therefore, blog layouts need more subheadings, graphics, and other indications of what information follows. (2) Onscreen reading is harder than reading printed paper, so legibility is crucial in blogs.

RULES AND RATIONALES FOR WRITING BLOGS

Expert web designer, copywriter, and blogger Annabel Cady (http://www.successfulblogging.com/) shares the following blog-posting rules: Format all posts for smooth page layout and easy scanning. Column width should be a maximum of 80 characters, including spaces, for easier reading. Headings and subheadings separate text visually, enable scanning or skimming, and encourage continued reading. Bullet-pointed or numbered lists enable quick information location and scanning. Punctuation is critical, so beginners should use shorter sentences until confident. Blog paragraphs should be far shorter—two to six sentences each—than paragraphs written on paper to enable "chunking" because reading onscreen is more difficult. Sans serif fonts are usually clearer than serif fonts, and larger font sizes are better. Highlight important material and draw attention with **boldface**, but avoid overuse. Avoid hard-to-read *italics* and ALL CAPITALS. Include enough blank spaces: overly busy blogs tire eyes and brains. Images not only break up text, but also emphasize and enhance text, and can attract initial reader attention. Use background colors judiciously to avoid distracting the eye or making it difficult to read. Be consistent throughout posts, since people read them in different orders. Tell a story with a beginning, middle, and end.

CONSIDERATIONS TO TEACH STUDENTS ABOUT OCCASIONS, PURPOSES, AND AUDIENCES

Teachers can explain to students that organizing their ideas, providing evidence to support the points they make in their writing, and correcting their grammar and mechanics are not simply for following writing rules or correctness for its own sake, but rather for ensuring that specific reader audiences understand what they intend to communicate. For example, upper-elementary-grade students writing for lower-elementary-grade students should write in print rather than script, use simpler vocabulary, and avoid writing in long, complex, compound, or complex-compound sentences. The purpose for writing guides word choice, such as encouraging readers to question opposing viewpoints or stimulate empathy and/or sympathy. It also influences narrative, descriptive, expository, or persuasive/argumentative format. For instance, business letters require different form and language than parent thank-you notes. Persuasive techniques, like words that evoke certain reader emotions, description that appeals to reader beliefs, and supporting information can all affect reader opinions.

QUESTIONS TO DETERMINE CONTENT AND FORMAT

When student writers have chosen a viewpoint or idea about which to write, teachers can help them select content to include and the writing format(s) most appropriate to their subject. They should have students ask themselves what their readers need to know to enable them to agree with the viewpoint in the writing, or to believe what the writer is saying. Students can imagine another

person hearing them say what they will write about, and responding, "Oh, yeah? Prove that!" Teachers should have students ask themselves what kinds of evidence they need to prove their positions/ideas to skeptical readers. They should have students consider what points might cause the reader to disagree. Students should consider what knowledge their reading audience shares in common with them. They should also consider what information they need to share with their readers. Teachers can have students adapt various writing formats, organizing techniques, and writing styles to different purposes and audiences to practice with choosing writing modes and language.

APPROPRIATE KINDS OF WRITING FOR DIFFERENT TASKS, PURPOSES, AND AUDIENCES

Students who are writing to persuade their parents to grant some additional privilege, such as permission for a more independent activity, should use more sophisticated vocabulary and diction that sounds more mature and serious to appeal to the parental audience. Students who are writing for younger children, however, should use simpler vocabulary and sentence structure, as well as choosing words that are more vivid and entertaining. They should treat their topics more lightly, and include humor as appropriate. Students who are writing for their classmates may use language that is more informal, as well as age-appropriate. Students wanting to convince others to agree with them should use persuasive/argumentative form. Those wanting to share an experience should use descriptive writing. Those wanting to relate a story and what can be learned from it should write narratives. Students can use speculative writing to invite others to join them in exploring ideas.

MAIN IDEAS, SUPPORTING DETAILS, AND OUTLINING A TOPIC

A writer often begins the first paragraph of a paper by stating the main idea or point, also known as the topic sentence. The rest of the paragraph supplies particular details that develop and support the main point. One way to visualize the relationship between the main point and supporting information is as a table: the tabletop is the main point, and each of the table's legs is a supporting detail or group of details. Both professional authors and students can benefit from planning their writing by first making an outline of the topic. Outlines facilitate quick identification of the main point and supporting details without having to wade through the additional language that will exist in the fully developed essay, article, or paper. Outlining can also help readers to analyze a piece of existing writing for the same reason. The outline first summarizes the main idea in one sentence. Then, below that, it summarizes the supporting details in a numbered list. Writing the paper then consists of filling in the outline with detail, writing a paragraph for each supporting point and adding an introduction and conclusion.

> **Review Video: Topics and Main Ideas**
> Visit mometrix.com/academy and enter code: 407801

WORDS THAT SIGNAL INTRODUCTION OF SUCCESSIVE DETAILS

When a paragraph opens with the topic sentence, the second sentence may begin with a phrase like "First of all," introducing the first supporting detail/example. The writer may introduce the second supporting item with words or phrases like "Also," "In addition," and "Besides." The writer might introduce succeeding pieces of support with wording like, "Another thing," "Moreover" "Furthermore," or "Not only that, but." The writer may introduce the last piece of support with "Lastly," "Finally," or "Last but not least." Writers get off the point by presenting "off-target" items not supporting the main point. For example, a main point "My dog is not smart" is supported by the statement, "He's six years old and still doesn't answer to his name." But "He cries when I leave for school" is not supportive, as it does not indicate lack of intelligence. Writers stay on point by presenting only supportive statements that are directly relevant to and illustrative of their main point.

44

PARAGRAPHS

A paragraph is a group of sentences that forms a unit separate from (but connected to) other paragraphs. Typically, all of one paragraph's sentences relate to one main idea or point. Two major properties that make paragraphs effective or ineffective are focus and development, or lack thereof. Paragraphs with poor focus impede comprehension because the sentences seem unrelated. When writers attempt to include too many ideas in a paragraph rather than focusing on the most important idea, or fail to supply transitions between ideas, they produce unfocused paragraphs. Undeveloped or inadequately-developed paragraphs may use good writing, but are still not effective. When a writer misunderstands the audience, depends overly on generalization, and fails to offer specific details, paragraph development will be poor. S/he may omit key term definitions, supporting evidence, setting description, context for others' ideas, background, and other important details, falsely assuming that readers already know these things.

WRITING EFFECTIVE PARAGRAPHS

The first thing a writer should do for a good paragraph is to focus on one main idea as the subject. A writer may introduce a paragraph by stating this main idea in a topic sentence. However, the main idea may be so obvious that writers can imply it rather than state it overtly and readers can easily infer it. Second, a writer should use specific details to develop the main idea. Details should capture readers' attention and also explain the author's ideas. Insufficient detail makes a paragraph too abstract, which readers find boring or confusing. Excessive detail makes a paragraph unfocused, which readers find overwhelming and also confusing. Third, a writer should develop paragraphs using structural patterns.

STRUCTURAL PATTERNS

Paragraphs have a nearly limitless range of structures, but certain patterns appear more often, including narration, description, definition, example and illustration, division and classification, comparison and contrast, analogy, cause and effect, and process.

NARRATION, DESCRIPTION, DEFINITION, EXAMPLE AND ILLUSTRATION, AND DIVISION AND CLASSIFICATION

In narration, a paragraph's main idea is developed with a story. Writers may use stories as anecdotal evidence to support the main point. In description, the writer constructs a clear image of a scene or event by including specific, sensory and other details that depict a person, thing, place, and/or time. Description shows readers instead of telling them. In definition, the writer provides a detailed explanation of a term that is central to the piece of writing. In example and illustration, the writer provides the readers with one or more examples that illustrate the point that the writer wants to make. Paragraphs using division divide a concept into its component parts—for example, body parts or experiment steps. Paragraphs using classification group separate things into categories by their similarities—such as mammals and insects, tragedies and comedies, and so on.

COMPARISON AND CONTRAST, ANALOGY, CAUSE AND EFFECT, AND PROCESS

Paragraphs that compare two or more things make note of their similarities. Paragraphs that contrast two or more things make note of how they differ. Another common paragraph technique is both comparing and contrasting two or more items within the same paragraph, showing both similarities and differences. Analogy compares two things in an unusual way, often things that belong to very different categories. This can afford new reader insight. Writers may use analogies to develop their ideas. Writers also develop their ideas in paragraphs through cause and effect, which either explains what caused some event or result, or shows the effects that something produced. Paragraphs may start with causes and proceed to effects, or begin with effects and then give causes. Process paragraphs describe and/or explain some process. They often sequence the stages, phases, or steps of the process using chronological order.

45

COHERENCE

When a paragraph is coherent, the details fit together so that readers can clearly understand the main point, and its parts flow well. Writers produce more coherent paragraphs when they select structural patterns appropriate to the conceptual content. There are several techniques writers can use to make paragraphs more coherent. Repetition connects sentences by repeating key words or phrases. This not only helps sentences flow together, but it also signals to readers the significance of the ideas these words and phrases communicate. Parallelism uses parallel structure, within or between sentences. Humorist Bill Maher once said, "We're feeding animals too sick to stand to people too fat to walk." His parallelism emphasized and connected two issues: the practice of using downed cows as food and the obesity epidemic. Consistency keeps the viewpoint, tone, and linguistic register consistent within the paragraph or piece. Finally, transitions via connective words and phrases aid coherence immensely.

TRANSITIONS

Transitions between sentences and paragraphs guide readers from idea to idea. They also indicate relationships between sentences and paragraphs. Writers should be judicious in their use of transitions, inserting them sparingly. They should also be selected to fit the author's purpose—transitions can indicate time, comparison, and conclusion, among other purposes.

> **Review Video: Transitions in Writing**
> Visit mometrix.com/academy and enter code: 233246

TRANSITIONAL WORDS AND PHRASES

Transitional words and phrases indicating time include: afterward, immediately, earlier, meanwhile, recently, lately, now, since, soon, when, then, until, before, etc. Transitions indicating sequence include: too, first, second, further, moreover, also, again, and, next, still, too, besides, and finally. Transitions specifying comparison include: similarly, in the same way, likewise, also, again, and once more. Transitions that indicate contrast include: but, although, despite, however, instead, nevertheless, on the one hand... on the other hand, regardless, yet, and in contrast. Transitions indicating examples include: for example, for instance, such as, to illustrate, indeed, in fact, and specifically. Transitions indicating cause and effect include: because, consequently, thus, therefore, then, to this end, since, so, as a result, if... then, and accordingly.

Transitions indicating place include: near, far, here, there, to the left/right, next to, above, below, beyond, opposite, and beside. Transitions expressing concession include: granted that, naturally, of course, it may appear, and although it is true that. Transitions showing repetition, summary, or conclusion include: as mentioned earlier, as noted, in other words, in short, on the whole, to summarize, therefore, as a result, to conclude, and in conclusion. These tell readers how a sentence relates to the previous ones, and directs their thinking across ideas.

> **Review Video: Transitional Words and Phrases**
> Visit mometrix.com/academy and enter code: 197796

INTRODUCTION

Because readers encounter the introduction first, a writer should design the introductory paragraph to capture interest. Introductions should state the main point, thesis, or topic sentence soon and logically. Introductions should also prepare readers for the content of the body. To do this, the topic should first be narrowed to a main idea. The writer should then determine which main points support the main idea, and decide how to order those points. Supporting details can then be organized in sequential order. Some techniques for sequencing include strongest-to-weakest or weakest-to-strongest, logical progression, or sequencing by association. A writer should compose a thesis statement, which may contain the plan for the piece's structure and organization. Then it is time to write the first draft of the body of the document, including transitions between sentences and paragraphs. Finally, the writer creates the introduction, focusing on engaging the reader, integrating the thesis into the introduction, and maintaining the document's organization and structure.

> **Review Video: Introduction**
> Visit mometrix.com/academy and enter code: 961328

BODY

In an essay's introduction, the writer establishes the thesis and may indicate how the rest of the piece will be structured. In the body of the piece, the writer elaborates upon, illustrates, and explains the thesis statement. How writers sequence supporting details and their choices of paragraph types are development techniques. Writers may give examples of the concept introduced in the thesis statement. If the subject includes a cause-and-effect relationship, the author may explain its causality. A writer will explain and/or analyze the main idea of the piece throughout the body, often by presenting arguments for the veracity or credibility of the thesis statement. Writers may use development to define or clarify ambiguous terms. Paragraphs within the body may be organized with natural sequences, like space and time. Writers may employ inductive reasoning, using multiple details to establish a generalization or causal relationship, or deductive reasoning, proving a generalized hypothesis or proposition through a specific example/case.

> **Review Video: Drafting Body Paragraphs**
> Visit mometrix.com/academy and enter code: 724590

CONCLUSION

Two important principles to consider when writing a conclusion are strength and closure. A strong conclusion gives the reader a sense that the author's main points are meaningful and important, and that the supporting facts and arguments are convincing, solid, and well developed. When a conclusion achieves closure, it gives the impression that the writer has stated what needed stating and completed the work, rather than simply stopping after a specified length. Some things to avoid when writing concluding paragraphs include: introducing a completely new idea, beginning with obvious or unoriginal phrases like "In conclusion" or "To summarize," apologizing for one's opinions or writing, repeating the thesis word for word rather than rephrasing it, and believing that the conclusion must always summarize the piece.

> **Review Video: Drafting Conclusions**
> Visit mometrix.com/academy and enter code: 209408

COHERENCE VS. COHESION

Cohesive writing flows smoothly, helping readers move easily from sentence to sentence and holding all sentences together. Coherent writing contains sentences that are not only clear individually, but also combine into a unified paragraph or passage. While we are often warned against using passive voice, sometimes a paragraph or passage is more cohesive using a passive construction that allows sentences to flow together better. For example, "Scientists are studying black holes. A black hole is made when a dead star collapses." The passive voice allows repetition of "black hole" from the end of the first sentence to the beginning of the second, connecting this idea. Making one sentence follow from the previous one is the "old-to-new" technique. If the second sentence in active voice read, "When a dead star collapses, it becomes a black hole," the term "black hole" would be farther away from the first sentence and they would not connect or flow as well.

Writers can make text cohesive with the old-to-new principle: starting sentences with familiar information and ending them with new or unexpected information. A paragraph can be cohesive, with ideas flowing smoothly from one sentence to the next, but still not coherent. For example, a writer may connect words or ideas between sentences, but change the subject with each new sentence. When writing is coherent, readers can make sense of paragraphs or passages because sentence ideas integrate into a unified whole with interrelated concepts. Coherent writing enables readers to easily recognize individual sentence topics and understand how they combine into a group of connected ideas. Readers feel more comfortable when sentence topics appear earlier in sentences, and when a sequence of sentences indicates the import of the entire paragraph or passage.

Beginning sentences with familiar information in short and simple phrases, keeping topics consistent, and making obvious transitions between ideas will help produce cohesive and coherent writing.

> **Review Video: <u>Methods to Obtain Coherence in Writing</u>**
> Visit mometrix.com/academy and enter code: 831344

WRITING STYLE AND LINGUISTIC FORM

Linguistic form encodes the literal meanings of words and sentences. It comes from the phonological, morphological, syntactic, and semantic parts of a language. Writing style consists of different ways of encoding the meaning and indicating figurative and stylistic meanings. Writers' stylistic choices accomplish three basic effects on their audiences: (1) they communicate meanings beyond linguistically dictated meanings, (2) they communicate the author's attitude, such as persuasive/argumentative effects accomplished through style, and (3) they communicate or express feelings. Within style, component areas include: narrative structure; viewpoint; focus; sound patterns; meter and rhythm; lexical and syntactic repetition and parallelism; writing genre; representational, realistic, and mimetic effects; representation of thought and speech; meta-representation (representing representation); irony; metaphor and other indirect meanings; representation and use of historical and dialectal variations; gender-specific and other group-specific speech styles, both real and fictitious; and analysis of the processes for inferring meaning from writing.

PERSUASIVE TECHNIQUES

To appeal using reason, writers present logical arguments, such as using "If... then... because" statements. To appeal to emotions, authors ask readers how they would feel about something or to put themselves in another's place, present their point as making them feel best, and tell readers how they should feel. To appeal to character, morality, or ethics, authors present their points to readers as the right or most moral choices. Authors cite expert opinions to show readers that someone very knowledgeable about the subject or viewpoint agrees. Testimonials, via anecdotes about or quotations, add support. Bandwagon appeals persuade readers that everybody else agrees with the author's views. Authors appeal to greed by presenting their choice as cheaper, free, and/or more valuable for less cost. They appeal to laziness by presenting their views as more convenient, easy, or relaxing. Authors also anticipate potential objections and argue against them before audiences think of them, thereby depicting those objections as weak.

Authors can use comparisons like analogies, similes, and metaphors to persuade audiences. For example, a writer might represent excessive expenses as "hemorrhaging" money, which the author's recommended solution will stop. Authors can use negative word connotations to make some choices unappealing to readers, and positive word connotations to make others more appealing. Using humor can relax readers and garner their agreement. However, writers must take care: ridiculing opponents works with readers who already agree, but otherwise can backfire by angering other readers. Rhetorical questions need no answer, but create effect that can force agreement, such as asking the question, "Wouldn't you rather be paid more than less?" Generalizations persuade readers by being impossible to disagree with; writers can make these appear to support their viewpoints, like saying, "We all want peace, not war" regarding more specific political arguments. Transfer and association persuade by example: if advertisements show attractive actors enjoying their products, audiences imagine they will experience the same. Repetition, can also sometimes effectively persuade audiences.

> **Review Video: Rhetorical Strategy of Persuasion**
> Visit mometrix.com/academy and enter code: 302658

CRITICAL EVALUATION OF EFFECTIVENESS OF PERSUASIVE METHODS

First, readers should identify the author's thesis—what s/he argues for or against. They should consider the argument's content and why the author saw a need to present it. Does the author offer solutions to problems raised? If so, are they realistic? Note all central ideas and evidence supporting the author's thesis. Research any unfamiliar subjects or vocabulary. Readers should then outline or summarize the work in their own words. Identify which type(s) of appeal(s) the author uses. Readers should evaluate how well the author communicated meaning from the reader's perspective: Did they respond to emotional appeals with anger, concern, happiness, etc.? If so, why? Decide if the author's reasoning sufficed for changing the reader's mind. Determine whether the content and presentation were accurate, cohesive, and clear. Readers should also ask themselves whether they found the author believable or not, and why or why not.

CLASSICAL AUTHOR APPEALS

In his *On Rhetoric,* ancient Greek philosopher Aristotle defined three basic types of appeal used in writing, which he called pathos, ethos, and logos. *Pathos* means suffering or experience and refers to appeals to the emotions (the English word "pathetic" comes from this root). Writing that is meant to entertain audiences, by making them either happy, as with comedy, or sad, as with tragedy, uses pathos. Aristotle's *Poetics* states that evoking the emotions of terror and pity is one of the criteria for writing tragedy. *Ethos* means character and connotes ideology (the English word "ethics" comes from this root). Writing that appeals to credibility, based on academic, professional, or personal merit uses ethos. *Logos* means "I say" and refers to a plea, opinion, expectation, word or speech, account, opinion, or reason. (The English word "logic" comes from this root.) Aristotle used it to mean persuasion that appeals to the audience through reasoning and logic to influence their opinions.

AUTHOR'S ARGUMENT IN ARGUMENTATIVE WRITING

When an author writes in argumentative mode, the argument is a belief, position, or opinion that the author wants to convince readers to believe as well. For the first step, readers should identify the issue. Some issues are controversial, meaning people disagree about them. Gun control, foreign policy, and the death penalty are all controversial issues. The next step is to determine the author's position on the issue. That position or viewpoint constitutes the author's argument. Readers should then identify the author's assumptions: things s/he accepts, believes, or takes for granted without needing proof. Inaccurate or illogical assumptions produce flawed arguments and can mislead readers. Readers should identify what kinds of supporting evidence the author offers—research results, personal observations or experiences, case studies, facts, examples, expert testimony and opinions, and comparisons. Readers should decide how relevant this support is to the argument.

The first three reader steps to evaluate an author's argument are to identify the author's assumptions, identify the supporting evidence, and decide whether the evidence is relevant. For example, if an author is not an expert on a particular topic, then that author's personal experience or opinion might not be relevant. The fourth step is to assess the author's objectivity. For example, consider whether the author introduces clear, understandable supporting evidence and facts to support the argument. The fifth step is evaluating whether the author's argument is complete. When authors give sufficient support for their arguments and also anticipate and respond effectively to opposing arguments or objections to their points, their arguments are complete. However, some authors omit information that could detract from their arguments. If instead they stated this information and refuted it, it would strengthen their arguments. The sixth step in evaluating an author's argumentative writing is to assess whether the argument is valid. Providing clear, logical reasoning makes an author's argument valid. Readers should ask themselves whether the author's points follow a sequence that makes sense, and whether each point leads to the next. The seventh step is to determine whether the author's argument is credible, meaning that it is convincing and believable. Arguments that are not valid are not credible, so step seven depends on step six. Readers should be mindful of their own biases as they evaluate and should not expect authors to conclusively prove their arguments, but rather to provide effective support and reason.

LOGICAL FALLACIES

Post hoc ergo propter hoc is Latin for "After this, therefore because of this." This equates to reasoning that because X happened before Y, X must have caused Y. But just as correlation does not imply causation, neither does chronological sequence. For example, one cannot assume that because most rapists read pornography as teenagers that pornography causes rape. A red herring is irrelevant information introduced to distract others from the pertinent issue. For example, one author claims that welfare dependence raises crime rates, while another argues plausibly that some increase in crime is justified in addressing poverty. However, if the second author argued instead, "But how can the poor survive without help?" that would be a red herring. Slippery slopes, when fallacious, are arguments that one event will cause others without demonstrating any cause-and-effect relationship—hence non-sequiturs. For example, arguing that legalizing one drug will cause all drugs to be legalized is obviously false. Straw man is refuting an exaggeration or caricature of someone's argument, not the real argument.

RATIONALES FOR KNOWING LOGICAL FALLACIES

For persuasive and argumentative writing, logic is necessary, but so are supporting facts, insights, and the plausibility of an argument. Although logic by itself may show that the answer to a question discussed is unknown, the most plausible argument can still convince audiences. One reason for knowing the names and processes of logical fallacies is enabling writers to identify flawed reasoning by those presenting opposing viewpoints—and identify them precisely by supplying a Latin name for each. Another reason is that by identifying logical fallacies, the author does not simply make an opponent's argument weaker or less convincing, but s/he actually eliminates it from the debate. Rather than counterarguments—allowing opponents' rhetoric proving their arguments' importance—this makes audiences question the validity, and even existence, of the opposing argument. If the other author cannot justify it strongly, that argument can be negated, and so the audience does not even consider it.

STEPS OR STRATEGIES TO DRAW ATTENTION TO LOGICAL FALLACIES IN OPPOSING ARGUMENTS

The writer should first restate the targeted opposing argument. Then s/he points out this argument is a logical fallacy and identifies it by name. The writer then explains the meaning of this logical fallacy and why it involves erroneous reasoning. Writers must not let their language become pompous or pedantic in tone during this explanation. Instead, they appeal more to audiences by stating the meaning of the fallacy as though their perceptive readers and listeners already know it. For example, if a writer identifies an opposing writer's use of an appeal to public opinion, s/he defines this by pointing out that majority agreement with a position does not make it right. Writers then give overt examples of a fallacy's incorrectness—such as historical beliefs that the world was flat or that slavery was acceptable. Finally, writers call for the erroneous argument to be ruled out, leaving their opponents with an untenable position.

Argumentum ad antiquitatem means an argument to tradition or antiquity. We have often read or heard this used when people write or say, "We have always done it this way." An example might be that the governments of all major societies have always supplied state funding for cultural pursuits and the arts. However, it is not logical that this intrinsically warrants continuing to do it. An inherent weakness of this argument is that others can refute it easily just by drawing attention to it. Therefore, it should not be a writer's first choice. If one feels the need to use this argument, one way to support it is to offer a reason for respecting the tradition cited. One might support arguing for a tradition with the evolutionary principle of natural selection—such as saying that the reason all known civilizations practice this tradition is because those that ignored it failed to survive.

Argumentum ad hominem is against the person, not the person's statements/ideas. The arguer attacks a person's motives or character, not what s/he wrote or said. This is less often by name-calling, such as "He is a communist/fascist/greedy capitalist," but more commonly by attacking the person as an information source. If one cites ending the Vietnam War, signing environmental laws, and opening China as positive accomplishments of Richard Nixon, and quotes him regarding free trade, then the *ad hominem* arguer might cite the Watergate scandal as evidence Nixon was a "crook" and liar, so nobody can believe anything he said. Arguments *ad hominem* also are used against people arguing for anything that would benefit them and against anything that would disadvantage them—like owners of corporate conglomerates arguing against anti-trust laws—shifting focus away from the argument's validity to focus on who makes it. Many *ad hominem* arguments may be restated about ideas versus people—such as not claiming someone is a fascist, but his/her position is.

Argumentum ad ignorantiam is an argument appealing to ignorance. In other words, the arguer presumes the truth of something based on its not being proven untrue. For example, one would do better by presenting actual data to prove climate change than by arguing it is true because nobody has proven it false. The burden of proof is a key factor for determining whether this argument is fallacious or not. As an analogy, in the United States legal system, a defendant is innocent until proven guilty—rather than guilty until proven innocent as in some other court systems. Thus defense attorneys can argue that their client is not guilty because the prosecution has not proven him/her guilty. However, prosecuting attorneys cannot argue that the defendant must be guilty of committing a crime because s/he has no alibi. Both arguments constitute *ad ignorantiam*, but in the American legal system, the burden of proof is on the prosecution rather than the defense. Similarly, in rhetoric, the proposer typically has the burden of proof.

The logical fallacy *argumentum ad logicam*, or argument/appeal to logic, presumes something is untrue based on an invalid argument or proof. This is fallacious because other, valid arguments could exist. The *argumentum ad logicam* frequently occurs within the context of the *straw man* fallacy, which argues against a distortion or exaggeration of a position, not the actual position. The *ad logicam* appeal is determined as fallacious or not through the burden of proof: If the proposer of the original position does not prove it, s/he loses the debate even though other arguments not presented could have proven it. Also, if one side disproves another's point as invalid, it will be judged invalid, regardless of whether the proposer could have proven it with a better argument because s/he did not do so; the burden of proof is on the proposer. This determination of fallacy or validity via burden of proof is comparable to that used with *argumentum ad ignorantiam*.

Argumentum ad misericordiam means argument/appeal to pity. This is often employed by those pleading to others for donations and other assistance to help starving children, abused animals, and poor people. Of course many pity such victims and want to help, but what makes this appeal illogical is that by itself, it cannot make expenses free, make true something untrue, or render something possible that is impossible. It is valid, however, to emphasize a problem's significance as a way of supporting one's proposing a particular solution to that problem. The proposer of the solution must then be able to address such objections as whether that solution is possible or feasible; what negative impacts it could have on others, even while providing positive impacts on those it would help; and its expenses and how to provide for those. Appealing to pity is acceptable to support arguments that a proposal's benefits justify its costs, but unacceptable as the sole response to objections without otherwise addressing them.

Argumentum ad nauseam translates literally as argument to the point of nausea. In other words, this tactic involves repeating one's point over and over until listeners are so disgusted that they cannot tolerate hearing it any longer. Reiterating a true statement over and over is not fallacious in itself, but expecting such repetition to replace actual logic is. Despite the absence of reasoning, repetition has a powerful effect of convincing listeners. This makes *argumentum ad nauseam* very popular. When one side in a spoken or written debate or controversy has used this technique of constant repetition without supplying any evidence to support or document the assertion, the other side can refute it by pointing out that the repeated statement has not been substantiated with any proof.

Argumentum ad numerum, translated as argument or appeal to numbers, is a rhetorical device of citing mathematical figures as "proof" that something is true. For example, one might argue, "80 percent of the public supports this legislation." The fallacy here is that the agreement of the majority does not make something true. The 80 percent of the public that supports a law could be wrong in doing so—like in the antebellum Southern United States, where the majority of the public supported slavery. They had considerable incentive to take this position to preserve the entire foundation of their economy and way of life, but they were not morally justified in doing so. *Argumentum ad numerum* resembles *argumentum ad populum*—appeal to popularity or to the people. Their minor difference is that arguing to the people appeals directly to the nearby public, while appealing to numbers attempts to persuade others based on citing how many other people agree. These are similar enough to be often used interchangeably in rhetoric.

The meaning of *argumentum ad verecundiam* is arguing or appealing to authority. This is attempting to prove one's position by citing the opinion of someone who is not an expert in the specific subject at issue. For example, Enrico Fermi and Albert Einstein were both pacifists, and objected strenuously to having their science applied for building bombs. While some agree and some do not, the fact is that Fermi and Einstein were experts in nuclear physics, but not in politics or foreign policy. Citing or quoting authorities in the subject under discussion, though, is not fallacious. It is also acceptable to quote a non-expert who nevertheless made an eloquent statement appropriate to one's argument. Unacceptable uses of the appeal to authority include using unqualified sources to verify facts and/or implying that a given position has to be correct just because a certain person believes it is.

Circulus in demonstrando is Latin for a circular argument. This means that by trying to use the assertion or idea they want to prove is itself a part of their proof, people using circular argumentation are actually "talking in circles." As an example, someone argues, "X is illegal. Because it is illegal, one should not do it. Because one shouldn't do it, the government should prevent people from doing it. This is why it is illegal." In this example, the circular nature of the argument is obvious. However, some arguments are circular but less easily recognized. Some politicians and political commentators are notorious for using circular arguments. To refute the fallacy of *circulus in demonstrando,* one can summarize the arguer's statement as "You are saying that X is true because X is true," and then additionally point out that the arguer has not provided any actual proof.

"Complex question" refers to a rhetorical tactic that implicitly presumes something as true before it has been established. An obvious example is when reporters or lawyers ask someone, "Have you stopped embezzling?" when there is no proof that the person questioned ever embezzled. This tactic is employed to trick people into admitting things they would not admit in direct questioning. A less obvious example is asking someone, "Since most African-Americans are poor, do you believe the measures proposed would be effective?" The first clause is not true, but the person questioned could be so focused on the second clause and how to answer it as to overlook the falsehood. This is more effective in spoken than written language: in real-time spoken interactions, it can confuse someone; in a written piece, the reader has time to reconsider it and realize it is untrue. A major drawback is that if the person questioned notices the falsehood and confronts the questioner, it makes the questioner appear foolish.

Cum hoc ergo propter hoc means in Latin, "With this, therefore because of this." In other words, because these occur together, one causes the other. A parallel fallacy in scientific research is assuming that correlation indicates causation. Things can occur together out of coincidence: people may attribute economic improvement to a certain president's administration when it may be more due to technological advances. Things can occur together, but one is an effect of prior causes: an improved economy during one president's administration can be the result of an earlier president's actions. Things can occur together and be unrelated to each other, but both related to a common reason: as an economic remedy, one president enacts downsizing measures, which many voters dislike, so they consequently elect a different president, and benefits of the previous president's downsizing appear after the election of the subsequent president. Whereas correlation can never mean causation in scientific research, in rhetoric one may attribute causation to correlation if one can provide sufficiently convincing reasons for it.

The Latin *dicto simpliciter* literally means "spoken simply," a figuratively sweeping generalization. When people make sweeping proclamations they presume are always true, they are stereotyping—which is another term for this. An example is generalizing that as a group, women are not as strong physically as men and assuming that therefore, they cannot serve equally in the military. While the first statement is true in general, it is not always true of specific individuals: some women are stronger than some men. In rhetoric, it is typically sufficient simply to state why a sweeping generalization does not prove someone's point without using the official terminology or pointing out its logical fallacy. Sweeping generalizations are understood by the public without instruction in rhetorical devices. Hence, experts also advise that naming the fallacy in Latin in this case seems condescending. Non-fallacious generalizations are always true individually, such as "Normal human females have two X chromosomes; normal human males have an X and a Y chromosome."

The appeal to nature assumes that anything natural or part of nature is good, and/or that anything not natural is bad. For example, some people may argue that birth control or homosexuality is wrong because these are not natural. In addition to the problem of defining the meaning of "natural," it is also illogical to equate "unnatural" or non-natural with wrong. Human beings use fire, construct and use tools, wear clothing, and farm the soil; these can be deemed "unnatural," yet they are both common and beneficial. Because of these inherent weaknesses, this argument is not effective. For instance, defending environmentalism only on the basis of preserving natural resources or wildernesses does not provide strong enough reasons. However, this can be defended more strongly by appealing to humans on the basis of their own survival by arguing that humans live within a complex ecosystem that is easily damaged by certain human activities which could destroy both the ecosystem and thus humanity as a part of it.

In the naturalistic fallacy, one draws conclusions regarding values—in other words, right and wrong or good and bad—based only on factual statements. This is fallacious because any logical inferences based on facts alone will constitute simply more statements of fact, rather than statements of value. A statement of value must be used together with facts to make a conclusion about values For instance, the statement, "This medication will keep you from dying" might seem to connect to a conclusion, "You should take this medication." However, the former is a statement of fact, the latter one of value. For the conclusion to be logically valid, an additional premise is needed, "You should do what you need to do to stay alive."

Argumentum ad antiquitatem, or appeal to tradition (something is right because it has always been done) and the appeal to nature (something is right because it is natural), are forms of the naturalistic fallacy: they draw conclusions about values using statements of fact without any statement(s) of value to connect logically with conclusions. Facts represent what is; values represent what ought to be. Philosopher David Hume described these fallacies as attempts to bridge the "is-ought gap." Initial axioms of value are not necessarily justifiable via pure logic. However, rhetoric is not limited to pure logic. Three ways to rebut an axiom of value, such as "Anything natural is good," are: (1) Ask if anybody—yourself, the judge of a debate, or even your opponent who stated it—truly believes this; (2) present another value axiom that competes with it, like "Anything that improves people's lives is good," so the judge is forced to choose between the two; and (3) cite logical ramifications of the statement's contradiction of basic morality.

In Latin, *non sequitur* means "It does not follow." If someone says, for instance, "Racism is wrong; thus affirmative action is necessary," this conclusion does not logically follow the initial premise. If one says instead, "Racism is wrong; affirmative action would decrease racism; thus affirmative action is needed," the logical connection is supplied. Some rhetoricians include *non sequiturs* in their opening arguments strategically to avoid giving away to their opponents a counterargument they anticipate. Except in the cases of significant, obvious counterarguments that should be anticipated and answered early, it is more strategic to wait for an opponent to raise an argument to rebut, rather than waste time and energy answering unstated objections. It is inadvisable to claim *non sequitur* whenever an opponent does not anticipate each of one's counterarguments. The best application for pointing out this fallacy is when an opponent attempts to show a causal chain without proving each link. Identifying each unsubstantiated step ultimately reveals such attempted chains as weak and implausible.

Petitio principii means "begging the question": when attempting to prove something, one assumes the same thing one wants to prove. In terms of logical structure, this is the same as using a circular argument. Although the meaning of "begging the question" is quite specific, many people misuse this term in rhetorical arguments. A question is begged if it is asked during a conversation but never answered, and meanwhile the parties in the discussion come to a conclusion about a related issue. For example, someone might argue, "Some people campaign for legalizing pornography because it is a medium for freedom of expression. However, this 'begs the question' of what freedom of expression means." This uses the term incorrectly. Some issues and discussions motivate questions rather than begging them. A more correct example of "begging the question" would be if someone argued, "Because we believe that pornography should be legalized, it constitutes a valid medium of free expression. Being free expression, it therefore should not be banned."

Translated from Latin, *tu quoque* means "you too." The old saying "Two wrongs don't make a right" addresses this fallacy. In rhetoric, one commits an error in logic—for example, making unproven claims—and defends it by rejoining that the opposition did the same. That both sides made the same error does not excuse either one. Though *tu quoque* is an obvious fallacy, it is often used to significant advantage in rhetoric: Disregarding whether any proposition is true or false, debaters can show which side made the better performance in arguing. For example, if both sides have equally appealed to audience pity (*argumentum ad misericordiam*), or both have used equal *ad hominem* arguments (attacking the person, not what s/he says), then to be fair a judge must penalize both equally, not just one. Additionally, it is not fallacious to show that "non-unique" advantages or disadvantages that apply equally to both sides cannot warrant preferring either position. *Tu quoque* can ensure that judging is only according to differentiating factors between sides.

> **Review Video: <u>Reading Logical Fallacies</u>**
> Visit mometrix.com/academy and enter code: 644845

English Language Conventions and Usage

PARTS OF SPEECH

Nouns are words for persons, places, or things. The words *girl, town*, and *house* are all nouns. Nouns are frequently the sentence subjects. Proper nouns are names. Pronouns replace nouns, including personal pronouns specifying person, number, gender, or case. Some common pronouns are *I, you, he, she, it, none,* and *which*. Personal pronouns may be subjective, such as sentence/clause subjects, or objective, like the objects of verbs or prepositions. Verbs are words for actions or states of being. Verbs are often sentence predicates. Adjectives are descriptive words modifying nouns, for example, *big* girl, *red* house, or other adjectives, such as *great* big house. Adverbs are descriptive words modifying verbs, adjectives, or other adverbs (including clauses), often ending in *–ly*. Examples include running *quickly* and *patiently* waiting. Conjunctive adverbs connect two clauses. The words *also, finally, however, furthermore, consequently, instead, meanwhile, next, still, then, therefore, indeed, incidentally,* and *likewise* are all conjunctive adverbs. Prepositions connect nouns/pronouns/phrases to other words in sentences, such as *on, in, behind, under, beside, against, beneath, over,* and *during*. Prepositional phrases include prepositions, their objects, and associated adjectives/adverbs. Conjunctions connect words/phrases/clauses. Common conjunctions include *and, when, but, or/nor, for, so,* and *yet*.

> **Review Video: Nouns and Pronouns**
> Visit mometrix.com/academy and enter code: 312073

FRAGMENTS AND RUN-ON SENTENCES

A sentence fragment is missing some essential component: a subject, predicate, or independent clause. An example of the latter is: "Although I knew that." This is incomplete because "although" makes it a dependent clause with no independent clause to complete the thought. By adding an independent clause, the sentence becomes complete: "Although I knew that, I forgot it." The statement "Going to dinner" has a subject (the gerund "going," a verbal functioning as a noun) and a prepositional phrase ("to dinner") but it does not have a proper subject. Again, adding a subject solves the problem: "We are going to dinner." To repair the statement "The friendly woman Mary," simply add a verb: "The friendly woman is Mary."

Run-on sentences lack necessary punctuation and/or connecting words: "We went to their party we had a very good time we plan to go again." This can be corrected several ways: "We went to their party. We had a very good time. We plan to go again." Or, less choppily: "We went to their party; we had a very good time, and we plan to go again."

> **Review Video: Fragments and Run-On Sentences**
> Visit mometrix.com/academy and enter code: 541989

COLONS VS. SEMICOLONS, ITS VS. IT'S, AND SAW VS. SEEN

Semicolons separate independent clauses, such as "She likes music; she likes to dance." Colons separate clauses when the second explains or illustrates the first: "She likes music: she likes to dance to it." People often misuse semicolons. For example, business letter salutations should use colons. "Dear Mr. Johnson:" is correct, while "Dear Mr. Johnson;" is not. Another common error is inserting an apostrophe into "its" to indicate possession. For example, the sentence, "The house is old; *its* paint is peeling" is correct. People often incorrectly spell this possessive personal pronoun as "it's." Their error is because some possessive nouns/pronouns use apostrophes, such as

"Barbara's idea" or "the man's hat." But "its," along with "yours," "hers," and "theirs" (without noun objects) do not. The only correct usage of "it's" is as a contraction of "it" and "is," as in "It's raining outside." "Saw" is the past tense of "to see." "Seen" is the perfect tense, used with auxiliary verbs to form present perfect "have seen," or past perfect, "had seen." This is why "I seen you" and "I have saw" are both incorrect.

PHRASES, CLAUSES, AND INDEPENDENT AND DEPENDENT CLAUSES

A clause has a subject and a predicate and the other elements of a sentence. An independent clause can stand on its own as a sentence. A dependent clause has a subject and a predicate, but it also has a subordinating conjunction, a relative pronoun, or some other connecting word or phrase that makes it unable to stand alone without an accompanying independent clause. For example, "I knew she was not at home" is an independent clause that can be a sentence on its own. But "because I saw her leave" is a dependent clause due to the subordinating conjunction "because," which makes it depend on the independent clause. The two clauses, joined together, form the complex sentence, "I knew she was not at home because I saw her leave." A phrase is neither a complete sentence nor a clause. It lacks a subject, or a predicate, or both. For example, "late at night" is an adverb phrase; "into the house" is a prepositional phrase. Phrases modify other sentence parts.

INCONSISTENT VERB TENSES AND NON-PARALLEL STRUCTURE

While changing verb tenses in writing can indicate temporal relationships, switching tenses in a sentence if both or all verbs represent the same time frame is incorrect. For example, "The professor explained the theory to students who ask questions" uses inconsistent verb tenses. The verbs should be either "explained" and "asked" or "explains" and "asks." It is also incorrect to maintain the same verb tense when the time frame shifts among actions. The sentence, "Before they even saw the evidence, they decided" should actually read, "Before they even saw the evidence, they *had* decided" because "decided" occurred prior to "saw." "Susie loves the puppy she adopted" is correct: present-tense "loves" is true currently, while past-tense "adopted" is something Susie did previously and is not doing currently. An example of non-parallel structure is: "She enjoys skating, skiing, swimming, and to sail a boat." Because the first three objects are all gerunds ("-ing" participles used as nouns), the fourth should be "sailing" to be consistent, not the inconsistent infinitive "to sail."

SIMPLE, COMPOUND, AND COMPLEX SENTENCES

A simple sentence is an independent clause. It states a complete thought and includes a subject and predicate/verb. An example is, "Some students cram before tests." "Students" is the subject; "some" is a modifying adjective. "Cram" is the verb; "before tests" is a modifying prepositional phrase. A compound sentence includes two independent clauses connected by a coordinator (*for, and, nor, but, or, yet, so*). For example, "Andrew likes history, but Cynthia prefers math" is a compound sentence. Independent clauses can also be joined by a semicolon instead of a coordinator: "Andrew likes history; Cynthia prefers math." A complex sentence has an independent clause and dependent clause, joined by a subordinator: "While Andrew likes history, Cynthia prefers math." The subordinating conjunction "while" makes the first clause dependent on the second. In the complex sentence, "Students are tired on exam day when they have crammed all night," the second clause, made subordinate by "when," depends on the independent clause that came first.

COMPOUND, COMPLEX, AND COMPOUND-COMPLEX SENTENCES

Compound sentences consist of two independent clauses, joined by a coordinating conjunction or punctuation like a semicolon, a colon, or sometimes a comma (for example, "He likes coffee, she likes tea"). Complex sentences consist of an independent clause and a dependent clause, connected by a subordinating word, making one clause subordinate to/dependent on the other. A compound-complex sentence includes two independent clauses, plus one or more dependent clauses. "Susan likes art, and Emily prefers science" is a compound sentence. "Although Susan likes art, Emily prefers science" is a complex sentence. An example of a compound-complex sentence is, "Susan, who draws well, likes art, but Emily, who is very methodical, prefers science." "Susan likes art" is an independent clause. "Who draws well" is a dependent clause with subordinator "who" modifying subject "Susan." "Emily prefers science" is another independent clause. "Who is very methodical" is another dependent clause with subordinator "who" modifying subject "Emily." "But" is the coordinating conjunction joining the two independent clauses.

Review Video: Variation of Sentence Types
Visit mometrix.com/academy and enter code: 845700

LIE VS. LAY

"To lie" is the infinitive form of the verb, as in "It is restful to lie down on a bed." Many people incorrectly use "lay down" instead. "To lay" is always a transitive verb, which means that it requires an object, and it means to make something lie down or to set something down, as in, "Lay that book on the table." The non-infinitive "lay" is the past tense of "to lie," e.g., "Yesterday I lay down." But the past tense of the transitive verb "to lay" is "laid," as in, "Yesterday I laid the book on the table." The present perfect and past perfect tenses of the intransitive verb "to lie" are both "lain," as in "I have lain here a long time" or "I had lain there all day before they came." However, the present and past perfect tenses of the transitive verb "to lay" are both "laid," as in "I have laid this book down for now" and "I had laid this book down last week."

COMPOUND WORDS

Compound words are words that consist of two single words that are used together to give a more specific meaning so commonly or often that they have been combined to form one word. These may be any part of speech, but are often nouns or adjectives. Some examples of nouns are *footsteps, heartbeat, countertop, gunshot, housewife, household, bookshelf, songbook, storybook, timetable, halfway, aftermath,* and *upkeep*. Some examples among adjectives include *paint-chipped, two-person, beat-up, pock-marked, war-torn, world-weary,* and *evidence-based*. Compound adjectives are often hyphenated, but not always, as in *bloodstained*. Also, authors may create compound adjectives when writing descriptively, as in *acne-scarred, hail-pitted,* and *flower-adorned,* to name a few.

DANGLING PARTICIPLES AND SQUINTING MODIFIERS

Dangling participles are common writing errors. They occur when someone writes a participial ("-ing") phrase followed by a clause, but the syntax makes the participle seemingly modify that clause when it really modifies something else that is unstated. Consider the following sentence, "Always getting into trouble, her life changes." The participle "getting" should modify an absent "she," but it incorrectly modifies "her life" instead. Her life is not always getting into trouble, she is. Or another example, "After eating his lunch, we left the restaurant." The dangling participle makes it sound as if we both ate his lunch. If the writer meant to indicate he ate, it should read, "After he ate his lunch, we left the restaurant." "Joanne's mother left when she was young" has a squinting modifier, making unclear who was young when the mother left—Joanne, her mother, or both. Possible corrections include: "When Joanne was young, her mother left," "Joanne's mother left as a young woman," or "Her young mother left when Joanne was a young child."

MISPLACED MODIFIERS

Misplaced modifiers are in the wrong part of a sentence, appearing to modify the wrong thing. For example, "This author creates a drama revolving around one character's journey in his new publication." This sounds like the new publication is a part of the character's journey. Correction involves moving the prepositional phrase: "In his new publication, this author creates a drama revolving around one character's journey."

Some other simple examples of how modifier placement affects meaning include: "She ate only fruit" versus "She only ate fruit." The first sentence means she ate nothing except fruit; the second means she did not plant, pick, wash, or cook fruit, but only ate it. Or, "He failed nearly every class he took" versus "He nearly failed every class he took." The former means he actually failed most of the classes he took, while the latter means he passed every class he took, but just barely. "Covered with flowers, she admired the field" means she was covered with flowers; "She admired the field covered with flowers" is correct.

> **Review Video: Misplaced Modifiers**
> Visit mometrix.com/academy and enter code: 312681

INCONSISTENT VERB TENSE

A narrative includes the following: "Anticipating the explosion, the insurgent watched the Humvees drive out of range. He frowned. Impatiently he jerks at the wire connected to the grenade's pin. But the handle was caught on something and had not detonated the grenade." This narrative switches tenses. To correct this, the verbs should be consistent in tense: "watched... frowned... jerked... was (caught)... had not detonated." Conversely, they could also be "watches... frowns... jerks... is (caught)... has not detonated." When the main narrative is in the past tense, the reference to something occurring earlier should be in the past perfect tense; when narrative is in the present tense, the reference should be in the present perfect tense.

PHRASES VS. CLAUSES AND TRANSITIVE VS. INTRANSITIVE VERBS

A clause makes a complete sentence, which can be just a subject and verb. However, the verb must be intransitive—one that does not require an object—for the sentence to be complete. For example, "I am," "I live," and "I love" are all complete sentences, but "I like" (or "I hate") is not because "like" needs an object—I like what? "I like it," "I like food," "I like to eat," and "I like eating" are all examples of complete sentences and independent clauses. A phrase lacks either a subject or a verb. For example, while "I like to go swimming" is a clause/sentence, "to go swimming" is a phrase: it has a verb but no subject. The imperative "Go now" is a complete sentence wherein the subject "you" is understood; the meaning is "[You] go now."

59

PUNCTUATION ERRORS IN POSSESSIVE PRONOUNS

Many people make the error of misspelling the possessive pronoun "its" as "it's" when the apostrophe is only ever used in the contraction of "it is," and never in the possessive. Another common error is misspelling other possessive pronouns by using apostrophes, such as "your's" and "her's." These are always incorrect. A possessive pronoun taking a noun as its object, such as "his hat," "your hat," or "her hat" is not complicated by any –s ending. However, when the possessive pronoun does not have any noun object, the –s ending is added: "It is hers," "That hat is yours," or "She is a friend of theirs." Just like other possessive pronouns without –s endings (such as "mine"), the possessive pronouns ending with –s never include an apostrophe.

DRAWBACKS TO WORDPROCESSING SPELL CHECKERS

Microsoft Word is one of the most popular word processing programs. It has many excellent features facilitating composition. However, students and other writers must realize that its spell checkers, and those of similar programs, are far from perfect. One cannot rely on them without paying attention to what they do. For example, a college student writing a paper on Sophocles' *Oedipus Rex* correctly typed the name of key character Laius, king of Thebes and father of Oedipus, throughout his paper. However, his spell checker, not recognizing the name, "corrected" it to Louis. The student only realized this at the last minute while on his way to class, paper in hand, without a computer or printer nearby, and he had to rewrite every instance of the name by hand. Spell checkers commonly fail to recognize proper names and foreign language words. To eliminate the red zigzag underline that Word uses to indicate a misspelling, simply right-click and select "Add to dictionary" from the drop-down menu. Students and writers must consciously proofread everything they write, rather than assume spell checkers are always correct.

Microsoft Word's grammar check identifies many common errors, but is often incorrect. It does not recognize reflexive verbs, such as "assess themselves" or "do it for themselves," and suggests changing "themselves" to "them." Many writers and students get perplexed when writing a complete sentence to find Word underlining it with a green zigzag, labeling it a "fragment." Sometimes this reflects a true error, like leaving the verb out of a clause. But other times, it makes no sense by current writing standards. Right-clicking, selecting "Grammar" from the drop-down menu, and selecting "Ignore rule" eliminates such wrong "corrections." (Another option is to simply ignore the markups.) If they have questions, writers and students can consult reputable grammar experts' websites about suspect "corrections."

The grammar checkers in popular word processing software programs like Microsoft Word can catch many inadvertent errors often caused by hurried typing and/or careless writing. However, these programs are not always correct, and in fact are often incorrect. Not only will Word's grammar checker incorrectly label some constructions incorrect when they are not, but it will also fail to identify other errors. For example, Noam Chomsky's famous sample sentence, "Colorless green ideas sleep furiously" is grammatically, morphologically, and syntactically correct in its construction, but makes no sense semantically—which was Chomsky's point. Grammar checkers are not people who can think, reason, and understand; they are simply programmed to identify certain things categorized as errors. So the grammar checker has no problem with Chomsky's sentence and does not flag anything in it as wrong. This is an example of how grammar checkers not only over-correct by identifying correct usages as incorrect, but also under-correct by not identifying incorrect usages. Writers and students must use their own judgment and knowledge and consult grammatical experts and/or their websites when needed.

Vocabulary and Syntax

DIALECT

Dialect is the form of a language spoken by people according to their geographical region, social class, cultural group, or any other distinctive group. It includes pronunciation, grammar, and spelling. Literary authors often use dialect when writing dialogue to illustrate the social and geographical backgrounds of specific characters, which supports character development. For example, in *The Adventures of Huckleberry Finn* (1885), Mark Twain's novel is written in the dialect of the young and uneducated white Southern character, opening with this sentence: "You don't know about me without you have read a book by the name of The Adventures of Tom Sawyer, but that ain't no matter." Twain uses a different and exaggerated dialect to represent the speech of the African-American slave Jim: "We's safe, Huck, we's safe! Jump up and crack yo' heels. Dat's de good ole Cairo at las', I jis knows it."

In *To Kill a Mockingbird,* author Harper Lee used dialect in the characters' dialogue to portray an uneducated boy in the American South: "Reckon I have. Almost died the first year I come to school and et them pecans—folks say he pizened 'em." Lee also uses many Southern regional expressions, such as "right stove up," "What in the sam holy hill?", "sit a spell," "fess" (meaning "confess"), "jim-dandy," and "hush your fussing." These contribute to Lee's characterization of the people she describes, who live in a small town in Alabama circa the 1930s. In *Wuthering Heights* (1847), Emily Bronte reproduces Britain's 18th-19th-century Yorkshire dialect in the speech of servant Joseph: "Running after t'lads, as usuald!... If I war yah, maister, I'd just slam t'boards i' their faces all on 'em, gentle and simple! Never a day ut yah're off, but yon cat o' Linton comes sneaking hither; and Miss Nelly, shoo's a fine lass!"

In addition to using dialects to support character development in novels, plays, poems, and other literary works, authors also manipulate dialects to accomplish various purposes with their intended reading audiences. For example, in an English Language Arts lesson plan for eighth graders (Groome and Gibbs, 2008), teachers point out author Frances O'Roark Dowell set her novel *Dovey Coe* (2000) in the Western North Carolina mountains of 1928. Dowell writes protagonist Dovey's narration in the regional Appalachian Mountain dialect to remind readers of the significance of the novel's setting. This lesson plan further includes two poems by African-American author Paul Laurence Dunbar: "When Malindy Sings" and "We Wear the Mask." Students are asked why Dunbar wrote the former poem in Southern slave dialect and the latter in Standard English. Exercises include identifying dialect/Standard English features, rewriting dialect in Standard English, identifying audiences, and identifying how author choices of dialects or Standard English affect readers and accomplish author purposes.

DIALECT VS. DICTION

When written as characters' dialogue in literary works, dialect represents the particular pronunciation, grammar, and figurative expressions used by certain groups of people based on their geographic region, social class, and cultural background. For example, when a character says, "There's gold up in them thar hills," the author is using dialect to add to the characterization of that individual. Diction is more related to individual characters than to groups of people. The way in which a specific character speaks, including his or her choice of words, manner of expressing himself or herself, and use of grammar all represent individual types of diction. For example, two characters in the same novel might describe the same action or event using different diction: One says "I'm heading uptown for the evening," and the other says "I'm going out for a night on the

town." These convey the same literal meaning, but due to their variations in diction they are expressed in different ways.

SIMPLE SURVEY RESEARCH INTO LINGUISTIC DIALECTS

To learn about different dialects spoken in different geographic regions, social classes, and cultural groups, students can undertake simple surveys of small groups of informants. Students should first make a list of words they have heard used in certain dialects. Then they can ask their respondents to identify the words they know. Students can also ask respondents to identify words they have heard of but cannot define. Using their lists of dialect words, students can ask informants to identify which words they use in their day-to-day conversations. For a more multidimensional survey, a student can ask the sampled informants all three questions—words that they know, those that they have heard of but do not know the meanings, and those that they use in their speech.

INFLUENCES ON REGIONAL DIALECT

Linguistic researchers have identified regional variations in vocabulary choices, which have evolved because of differences in local climates and how they influence human behaviors. For example, in the Southern United States, the Linguistic Atlas of the Gulf States (LAGS) Project by Dr. Lee Pederson of Emory University discovered and documented that people living in the northern or Upland section of the Piedmont plateau region call the fungal infection commonly known as athlete's foot "toe itch," but people living in the southern or Lowland section call it "ground itch." The explanation for this difference is that in the north, temperatures are cooler and people accordingly wear shoes, so they associate the itching with the feet in their description, but in the south, temperatures are hotter and people traditionally went barefoot, so they associated the itching with the ground that presumably transmitted the infection.

AFFIXES

Affixes in the English language are morphemes that are added to words to create related but different words. Derivational affixes form new words based on and related to the original words. For example, the affix *–ness* added to the end of the adjective *happy* forms the noun *happiness*. Inflectional affixes form different grammatical versions of words. For example, the plural affix *–s* changes the singular noun *book* to the plural noun *books*, and the past tense affix *–ed* changes the present tense verb *look* to the past tense *looked*. Prefixes are affixes placed in front of words. For example, *heat* means to make hot; *preheat* means to heat in advance. Suffixes are affixes placed at the ends of words. The *happiness* example above contains the suffix *–ness*. Circumfixes add parts both before and after words, such as how *light* becomes *enlighten* with the prefix *en-* and the suffix *–en*. Interfixes create compound words via central affixes: *speed* and *meter* become *speedometer* via the interfix *–o–*.

WORD ROOTS, PREFIXES, AND SUFFIXES TO HELP DETERMINE MEANINGS OF WORDS

Many English words were formed from combining multiple sources. For example, the Latin *habēre* means "to have," and the prefixes *in-* and *im-* mean a lack or prevention of something, as in *insufficient* and *imperfect*. Latin combined *in-* with *habēre* to form *inhibēre,* whose past participle was *inhibitus*. This is the origin of the English word *inhibit,* meaning to prevent from having. Hence by knowing the meanings of both the prefix and the root, one can decipher the word meaning. In Greek, the root *enkephalo-* refers to the brain. Many medical terms are based on this root, such as encephalitis and hydrocephalus. Understanding the prefix and suffix meanings (*-itis* means inflammation; *hydro-* means water) allows a person to deduce that encephalitis refers to brain inflammation and hydrocephalus refers to water (or other fluid) on the brain

PREFIXES

While knowing prefix meanings helps ESL and beginning readers learn new words, other readers take for granted the meanings of known words. However, prefix knowledge will also benefit them for determining meanings or definitions of unfamiliar words. For example, native English speakers and readers familiar with recipes know what *preheat* means. Knowing that *pre-* means in advance can also inform them that *presume* means to assume in advance, that *prejudice* means advance judgment, and that this understanding can be applied to many other words beginning with *pre-*. Knowing that the prefix *dis-* indicates opposition informs the meanings of words like *disbar, disagree, disestablish,* and many more. Knowing *dys-* means bad, impaired, abnormal, or difficult informs *dyslogistic, dysfunctional, dysphagia,* and *dysplasia.*

SUFFIXES

In English, certain suffixes generally indicate both that a word is a noun, and that the noun represents a state of being or quality. For example, *-ness* is commonly used to change an adjective into its noun form, as with *happy* and *happiness, nice* and *niceness,* and so on. The suffix *–tion* is commonly used to transform a verb into its noun form, as with *converse* and *conversation or move* and *motion.* Thus, if readers are unfamiliar with the second form of a word, knowing the meaning of the transforming suffix can help them determine meaning.

CONTEXT CLUES TO HELP DETERMINE MEANINGS OF WORDS

If readers simply bypass unknown words, they can reach unclear conclusions about what they read. However, if they look for the definition of every unfamiliar word in the dictionary, it can slow their reading progress. Moreover, the dictionary may list multiple definitions for a word, so readers must search the word's context for meaning. Hence context is important to new vocabulary regardless of reader methods. Four types of context clues are examples, definitions, descriptive words, and opposites. Authors may use a certain word, and then follow it with several different examples of what it describes. Sometimes authors actually supply a definition of a word they use, which is especially true in informational and technical texts. Authors may use descriptive words that elaborate upon a vocabulary word they just used. Authors may also use opposites with negation that help define meaning.

EXAMPLES AND DEFINITIONS

An author may use a word and then give examples that illustrate its meaning. Consider this text: "For students who are deaf or hard of hearing, teachers who do not know how to use sign language can help them understand certain instructions by using gestures instead, like pointing their fingers to indicate which direction to look or go; holding up a hand, palm outward, to indicate stopping; holding the hand(s) flat, palm(s) up, curling a finger toward oneself in a beckoning motion to indicate 'come here'; or curling all fingers toward oneself repeatedly to indicate 'come on', 'more', or 'continue.'" The author of this text has used the word "gestures" and then followed it with examples, so a reader unfamiliar with the word could deduce from the examples that "gestures" means "hand motions." Readers can find examples by looking for signal words "for example," "for instance," "like" "such as," and "e.g."

While readers sometimes have to look for definitions of unfamiliar words in a dictionary and/or do some work to determine a word's meaning from its surrounding context, at other times an author may make it easier for readers by defining certain words. For example, an author may write, "The company did not have sufficient capital, that is, available money, to continue operations." The author defined "capital" as "available money," and heralded the definition with the phrase "that is." Another way that authors supply word definitions is with appositives. Rather than being introduced by a signal phrase like "that is," "namely," or "meaning," an appositive comes after the vocabulary word it defines and is enclosed within two commas. For example, an author may write, "The Indians introduced the Pilgrims to pemmican, cakes they made of lean meat dried and mixed with fat, which proved greatly beneficial to keep settlers from starving while trapping." In this example, the appositive phrase following "pemmican" and preceding "which" defines the word "pemmican."

DESCRIPTIONS

When readers encounter a word they do not recognize in a text, the author may expand on that word to illustrate it better. While the author may do this to make the prose more picturesque and vivid, the reader can also take advantage of this description to provide context clues to the meaning of the unfamiliar word. For example, an author may write, "The man sitting next to me on the airplane was obese. His shirt stretched across his vast expanse of flesh, strained almost to bursting." The descriptive second sentence elaborates on and helps to define the previous sentence's word "obese" to mean extremely fat. One author described someone who was obese simply, yet very descriptively, as "an epic in bloat." A reader unfamiliar with the word "repugnant" can decipher its meaning through an author's accompanying description: "The way the child grimaced and shuddered as he swallowed the medicine showed that its taste was particularly repugnant."

OPPOSITES

Text authors sometimes introduce a contrasting or opposing idea before or after a concept they present. They may do this to emphasize or heighten the idea they present by contrasting it with something that is the reverse. However, readers can also use these context clues to understand familiar words. For example, an author may write, "Our conversation was not cheery. We sat and talked very solemnly about his experience, and a number of similar events." The reader who is not familiar with the word "solemnly" can deduce by the author's preceding use of "not cheery" that "solemn" means the opposite of cheery or happy, so it must mean serious or sad. Or if someone writes, "Don't condemn his entire project because you couldn't find anything good to say about it," readers unfamiliar with "condemn" can understand from the sentence structure that it means the opposite of saying anything good, so it must mean reject, dismiss, or disapprove. "Entire" adds another context clue, meaning total or complete rejection.

SYNTAX TO DETERMINE PART OF SPEECH AND MEANINGS OF WORDS

Syntax refers to sentence structure and word order. Suppose that a reader encounters an unfamiliar word when reading a text. To illustrate, consider an invented word like "splunch." If this word is used in a sentence like "Please splunch that ball to me," the reader can assume from syntactic context that "splunch" is a verb. We would not use a noun, adjective, adverb, or preposition with the object "that ball," and the prepositional phrase "to me" further indicates "splunch" represents an action. However, in the sentence, "Please hand that splunch to me," the reader can assume that "splunch" is a noun. Demonstrative adjectives like "that" modify nouns.

Also, we hand someone some*thing*—a thing being a noun; we do not hand someone a verb, adjective, or adverb. Some sentences contain further clues. For example, from the sentence, "The princess wore the glittering splunch on her head," the reader can deduce that it is a crown, tiara, or something similar from the syntactic context, without knowing the word.

SYNTAX TO INDICATE DIFFERENT MEANINGS OF SIMILAR SENTENCES

The syntax, or structure, of a sentence affords grammatical cues that aid readers in comprehending the meanings of words, phrases, and sentences in the texts that they read. Seemingly minor differences in how the words or phrases in a sentence are ordered can make major differences in meaning. For example, two sentences can use exactly the same words but have different meanings based on the word order: (1) "The man with a broken arm sat in a chair." (2) "The man sat in a chair with a broken arm." While both sentences indicate that a man sat in a chair, differing syntax indicates whether the man's or chair's arm was broken.

NUANCES OF WORD MEANING RELATIVE TO CONNOTATION, DENOTATION, DICTION, AND USAGE

A word's denotation is simply its objective dictionary definition. However, its connotation refers to the subjective associations, often emotional, that specific words evoke in listeners and readers. Two or more words can have the same dictionary meaning, but very different connotations. Writers use diction (a style element) to convey various nuances of thought and emotion by selecting synonyms for other words that best communicate the associations they want to trigger for readers. For example, a car engine is naturally greasy; in this sense, "greasy" is a neutral term. But when a person's smile, appearance, or clothing is described as "greasy," it has a negative connotation. Because of usages that have occurred in recent times, many words have gained additional and/or different meanings. The word "gay" originally meant happy or festive, as in the Christmas carol "Deck the Halls" lyrics, "Don we now our gay apparel," but in the 20th century, it also came to indicate a sexual preference.

> **Review Video: Denotation and Connotation**
> Visit mometrix.com/academy and enter code: 310092
>
> **Review Video: Word Usage**
> Visit mometrix.com/academy and enter code: 197863

FIGURES OF SPEECH

A figure of speech is a verbal expression whose meaning is figurative rather than literal. For example, the phrase "butterflies in the stomach" does not refer to actual butterflies in a person's stomach. It is a metaphor representing the fluttery feelings experienced when a person is nervous or excited—or when one "falls in love," which does not mean physically falling. "Hitting a sales target" does not mean physically hitting a target with arrows as in archery; it is a metaphor for meeting a sales quota. "Climbing the ladder of success" metaphorically likens advancing in one's career to ascending ladder rungs. Similes, such as "light as a feather" (meaning very light, not a feather's actual weight), and hyperbole, like "I'm starving/freezing/roasting," are also figures of speech.

> **Review Video: Figure of Speech**
> Visit mometrix.com/academy and enter code: 111295

World Literature

HISTORICAL BACKGROUND FOR ENGLISH LITERATURE

The ancient Greek Athenian elite were a highly educated society, developing philosophies and writing about principles for creating poetry and drama. During the Roman Empire, the Romans assimilated and adapted the culture of the Greeks they conquered into their own society. For example, the gods of Roman mythology were essentially the same as in Greek myth, only renamed in Latin. However, after the fall of the Roman Empire, the many European countries formerly united under Roman rule became fragmented. There followed a 1,000-year period of general public ignorance and illiteracy—called the Dark Ages as well as the Middle Ages. Only the Church remained a bastion of literacy: monks and priests laboriously copied manuscripts one at a time by hand. Johannes Gutenberg's 1450 invention of the movable-type printing press changed everything: multiple copies of books could be printed much faster. This enabled a public return to literacy, leading to the Renaissance, or "rebirth"—reviving access and interest for Greek and Roman classics, and generating a creative explosion in all arts.

MEDIEVAL POETRY

The medieval time period was heavily influenced by Greek and Latin Stoic philosophies. Medieval Christians appreciated Greek and Latin Stoic philosophies for their assigning more importance to spiritual virtues than material. Pagan stoic values were often adapted to Christian beliefs, and these were incorporated into early English literature.

GEOFFREY CHAUCER
THE CANTERBURY TALES

Medieval poet Geoffrey Chaucer (c. 1343-1400), called the "Father of English Literature," chiefly wrote long narrative poems, including *The Book of the Duchess, Anelida and Arcite, The House of Fame, The Parlement of Foules, The Legend of Good Women,* and *Troilus and Criseyde.* His most famous work is *The Canterbury Tales.* Its historical and cultural context is life during the Middle Ages, representing a cross-section of society—tradespeople, professionals, nobility, clergy, and housewives, among others—and religious pilgrimages, a common practice of the time. Its literary context is a frame-tale, a story within a story. Chaucer described a varied group of pilgrims on their way to Canterbury to visit the shrine of St. Thomas à Becket, taking turns telling stories to amuse the others. Tales encompass a broad range of subjects: bawdy comedy, chivalry, romance, and religion. These include *The Knight's Tale, The Miller's Tale, The Reeve's Tale, The Cook's Tale, The Man of Law's Tale, The Wife of Bath's Tale, The Friar's Tale, The Summoner's Tale, The Clerk's Tale, The Merchant's Tale, The Squire's Tale, The Franklin's Tale, The Physician's Tale, The Pardoner's Tale,* and *The Nun's Priest's Tale.*

THE PARLEMENT OF FOULES

In the brief preface to his poem "The Parlement of Foules," Chaucer refers to classic Roman author Cicero's "The Dream of Scipio," a dream-vision dialogue reflecting Stoic philosophy. Chaucer takes Cicero's broad scope of macrocosm (viewing the universe as a whole) and narrows it to a microcosm (individual focus) as he explores themes of order, disorder, and the role of humanity in nature. By using animals as characters, he is able to both parody and probe human nature for the reader.

66

SIR THOMAS BROWNE

Sir Thomas Browne (1605-1682) had an immeasurable influence on the development of English literature. Both his writing style and thought process were highly original. The Oxford English Dictionary credits Browne with coining over 100 new words (and quotes him in over 3,000 other entries), such as approximate, literary, and ultimate. His creativity and vision have inspired other authors over the past four centuries and were instrumental in developing much of the vocabulary used in today's prose and poetry. In 1671 he was knighted by Charles II in recognition of his accomplishments, which continue to affect literature today.

METAPHYSICAL POETS

Dr. Samuel Johnson, a famous 18th-century figure, who wrote philosophy, poetry, and authoritative essays on literature, coined the term "Metaphysical Poets" to describe a number of mainly 17th-century lyric poets who shared certain elements of content and style in common. The poets included John Donne (considered the founder of the Metaphysical Poets), George Herbert, Andrew Marvell, Abraham Cowley, John Cleveland, Richard Crashaw, Thomas Traherne, and Henry Vaughan. These poets encouraged readers to see the world from new and unaccustomed perspectives by shocking and surprising them with paradox; contradictory imagery; original syntax; combinations of religious, philosophical, and artistic images; subtle argumentation; and extended metaphors called conceits. Unlike their contemporaries, they did not allude to classical mythology or nature imagery in their poetry, but to current geographical and scientific discoveries. Some, like Donne, showed Neo-Platonist influences—like the idea that a lover's beauty reflected Eternity's perfect beauty. They were called metaphysical for their transcendence—Donne in particular—of typical 17th-century rationalism's hierarchical organization through their adventurous exploration of religion, ideas, emotions, and language.

ROMANTICISM

The height of the Romantic movement occurred in the first half of the 19th century. It identified with and gained momentum from the French Revolution (1789) against the political and social standards of the aristocracy and its overthrowing of them. Romanticism was also part of the Counter-Enlightenment, a reaction of backlash against the Enlightenment's insistence on rationalism, scientific treatment of nature, and denial of emotionalism. Though expressed most overtly in the creative arts, Romanticism also affected politics, historiography, natural sciences, and education. Though often associated with radical, progressive, and liberal politics, it also included conservatism, especially in its influences on increased nationalism in many countries. The Romantics championed individual heroes, artists, and pioneers; freedom of expression; the exotic; and the power of the individual imagination. American authors Edgar Allan Poe and Nathaniel Hawthorne, Laurence Sterne in England, and Johann Wolfgang von Goethe in Germany were included among well-known Romantic authors. The six major English Romantic poets were William Blake, William Wordsworth, Samuel Taylor Coleridge, Lord Byron, Percy Bysshe Shelley, and John Keats.

WILLIAM BLAKE

William Blake (1757-1827) is considered one of the earliest and foremost English Romantic poets. He was also an artist and printmaker. In addition to his brilliant poetry, he produced paintings, drawings, and engravings, impressive for their technical expertise, artistic beauty, and spiritual subject matter. Because he held many idiosyncratic opinions, and moreover because he was subject to visions, reporting that he saw angels in the trees and other unusual claims, Blake was often thought crazy by others during his life. His work's creative, expressive character, and its mystical and philosophical elements, led people to consider him both precursor to and member of

Romanticism, and a singular, original, unclassifiable artist at the same time. Blake illustrated most of his poetry with his own hand-colored, illuminated printing. His best-known poetry includes *Songs of Innocence and of Experience*, *The Book of Thel*, *The Marriage of Heaven and Hell*, and *Jerusalem*.

WILLIAM WORDSWORTH

William Wordsworth (1770-1850) was instrumental in establishing Romanticism when he and Samuel Taylor Coleridge collaboratively published *Lyrical Ballads* (1798). Wordsworth's "Preface to Lyrical Ballads" is considered a manifesto of English Romantic literary theory and criticism. In it, Wordsworth described the elements of a new kind of poetry, which he characterized as using "real language of men" rather than traditional 18th-century poetic style. In this Preface he also defined poetry as "the spontaneous overflow of powerful feelings [which] takes its origin from emotion recollected in tranquility." *Lyrical Ballads* included the famous works "The Rime of the Ancient Mariner" by Coleridge, and "Tintern Abbey" by Wordsworth. His semi-autobiographical poem, known during his life as "the poem to Coleridge," was published posthumously, entitled *The Prelude* and regarded as his major work. Wordsworth was England's Poet Laureate from 1843-1850. Among many others, his poems include "I Wandered Lonely as a Cloud" (often called "Daffodils"), "Ode: Intimations of Immortality," "Westminster Bridge," and "The World Is Too Much with Us."

SAMUEL TAYLOR COLERIDGE

Samuel Taylor Coleridge (1772-1834) was also a philosopher and literary critic and collaborated with William Wordsworth in launching the Romantic movement. He wrote very influential literary criticism, including the major two-volume autobiographical, meditative discourse *Biographia Literaria* (1817). Coleridge acquainted English-language intellectuals with German idealist philosophy. He also coined many now familiar philosophical and literary terms, like "the willing suspension of disbelief," meaning that readers would voluntarily withhold judgment of implausible stories if their authors could impart "human interest and a semblance of truth" to them. He strongly influenced the American Transcendentalists, including Ralph Waldo Emerson. Coleridge's poem *Love*, a ballad (written to Sara Hutchinson), inspired John Keats' poem "La Belle Dame Sans Merci." He is credited with the origin of "Conversational Poetry" and Wordsworth's adoption of it. Some of his best-known works include "The Rime of the Ancient Mariner," "Christabel," "Kubla Khan," "The Nightingale," "Dejection: An Ode," and "To William Wordsworth."

GEORGE GORDON, LORD BYRON

George Gordon Byron, commonly known as Lord Byron (1788-1824) is known for long narrative poems "Don Juan," "Childe Harold's Pilgrimage," and the shorter lyric poem "She Walks in Beauty." The aristocratic Byron travelled throughout Europe, living in Italy for seven years. He fought in the Greek War of Independence against the Ottoman Empire, making him a national hero in Greece, before dying a year later from a fever contracted there. He was the most notoriously profligate and flamboyant Romantic poet, with reckless behaviors including multiple bisexual love affairs, adultery, rumored incest, self-exile, and enormous debts. He became friends with fellow Romantic writers Percy Bysshe Shelley, the future Mary Shelley, and John Polidori. Their shared fantasy writing at a Swiss villa the summer of 1816 resulted in Mary Shelley's *Frankenstein*, Byron's *Fragment of a Novel*, and was the inspiration for Polidori's *The Vampyre*, establishing the romantic vampire genre. Byron also wrote linguistic volumes on American and Armenian grammars. His name is synonymous today with the mercurial Romantic.

PERCY BYSSHE SHELLEY

Percy Bysshe Shelley (1792-1822) was not famous during life but became so after death, particularly for his lyric poetry. His best-known works include "Ozymandias," "Ode to the West

Wind," "To a Skylark," "Music," "When Soft Voices Die," "The Cloud," "The Masque of Anarchy"; longer poems "Queen Mab"/"The Daemon of the World" and "Adonaïs"; and the verse drama *Prometheus Unbound.* Shelley's second wife, Mary Shelley, was the daughter of his mentor William Godwin and the famous feminist Mary Wollstonecraft (*A Vindication of the Rights of Woman*), and became famous for her Gothic novel *Frankenstein.* Early in his career Shelley was influenced by William Wordsworth's Romantic poetry, and wrote the long poem *Alastor, or the Spirit of Solitude.* Soon thereafter he met Lord Byron, and was inspired to write "Hymn to Intellectual Beauty". He composed "Mont Blanc," inspired by touring the French Alpine commune Chamonix-Mont-Blanc. Shelley also encouraged Byron to compose his epic poem *Don Juan.* Shelley inspired Henry David Thoreau, Mahatma Gandhi, and others to civil disobedience, nonviolent resistance, vegetarianism, and animal rights.

JOHN KEATS

John Keats (1795-1821), despite his short life, was a major English Romantic poet. He is known for his six Odes: "Ode on a Grecian Urn," "Ode on Indolence," "Ode on Melancholy," "Ode to a Nightingale," "Ode to Psyche," and "To Autumn." Other notable works include the sonnet "O Solitude," "Endymion," "La Belle Dame Sans Merci," "Hyperion," and the collection *Lamia, Isabella, The Eve of St. Agnes and Other Poems.* The intensity and maturity he achieved in only six years are often praised since his death, though during life he felt he accomplished nothing lasting. He wrote a year before dying, "I have left no immortal work behind me—nothing to make my friends proud of my memory—but I have lov'd the principle of beauty in all things, and if I had had time I would have made myself remember'd." He was proven wrong. His verse from "Ode on a Grecian Urn" is renowned: "'Beauty is truth, truth beauty'—that is all / Ye know on earth, and all ye need to know."

MODERNISM IN YEATS' POETRY

William Butler Yeats (1865-1939) was among the greatest influences in 20th-century English literature and was believed transitional from Romanticism to Modernism. His earlier verses were lyrical, but later became realistic, symbolic, and apocalyptic. He was fascinated with Irish legend, occult subjects, and historical cycles—"gyres." He incorporated Irish folklore, mythology, and legends in "The Stolen Child," "The Wanderings of Oisin," "The Death of Cuchulain," "Who Goes with Fergus?" and "The Song of Wandering Aengus." Early collections included *The Secret Rose* and *The Wind Among the Reeds.* His later, most significant poetry collections include *The Green Helmet, Responsibilities, The Tower,* and *The Winding Stair.* Yeats's visionary, apocalyptic poem "The Second Coming" (1920) reflects his belief that his times were the anarchic end of the Christian cycle/gyre: "what rough beast, its hour come round at last, / Slouches toward Bethlehem to be born?"

SAT Practice Test 1

Questions 1-6 pertain to the following passage:

Ithaca, C. P. Cavafy (1911)

When you start on your journey to Ithaca,
then pray that the road is long,
full of adventure, full of knowledge.
Do not fear the Lestrygonians
and the Cyclops and the angry Poseidon.
You will never meet such as these on your path,
if your thoughts remain lofty, if a fine
emotion touches your body and your spirit.
You will never meet the Lestrygonians,
the Cyclops and the fierce Poseidon,
if you do not carry them within your soul,
if your soul does not raise them up before you.

Then pray that the road is long.
That the summer mornings are many,
that you will enter ports seen for the first time
with such pleasure, with such joy!
Stop at Phoenician markets,
and purchase fine merchandise,
mother-of-pearl and corals, amber and ebony,
and pleasurable perfumes of all kinds,
buy as many pleasurable perfumes as you can;
visit hosts of Egyptian cities,
to learn and learn from those who have knowledge.

Always keep Ithaca fixed in your mind.
To arrive there is your ultimate goal.
But do not hurry the voyage at all.
It is better to let it last for long years;
and even to anchor at the isle when you are old,
rich with all that you have gained on the way,
not expecting that Ithaca will offer you riches.

Ithaca has given you the beautiful voyage.
Without her you would never have taken the road.
But she has nothing more to give you.
And if you find her poor, Ithaca has not defrauded you.
With the great wisdom you have gained, with so much experience,
you must surely have understood by then what Ithacas mean.

1. The poem is a metaphor for

    a. A trip to the Middle East
    b. Young love
    c. The passage of adolescence
    d. The journey of life
    e. Courage in battle

2. The poem draws on many allusions from which famous work?

    a. The Bible
    b. Homer's The Odyssey
    c. Aeschylus' Oresteia
    d. Xenophon's Anabasis
    e. Sophocles' Oedipus the King

3. What message does this passage imply?

> "Ithaca has given you the beautiful voyage.
> Without her you would never have taken the road.
> But she has nothing more to give you."

    a. People will always disappoint you.
    b. Trips are not worth the trouble.
    c. You will meet with many obstacles in life.
    d. You should make your travel plans early.
    e. It's about the journey, not the destination.

4. The poem is written in

    a. Second-person imperative
    b. First person
    c. Third person
    d. First-person plural
    e. Second-person plural

5. The message of the second stanza of the poem is to

    a. Enjoy the fruits of your labor
    b. Enjoy family and friendships
    c. Enjoy beauty, culture, knowledge, and education
    d. Enjoy an accumulation of gifts
    e. Enjoy trips to other cities

6. What does "her" in line 2 refer to?

> "Ithaca has given you the beautiful voyage.
> Without her you would never have taken the road.
> But she has nothing more to give you."

    a. The voyage
    b. Your partner
    c. Your mother
    d. Ithaca
    e. Your life

Questions 7-12 pertain to the following passage:

The Mill on the Floss, George Eliot (1860)

Chapter 1

Outside Dorlcote Mill

A wide plain, where the broadening Floss hurries on between its green banks to the sea, and the loving tide, rushing to meet it, checks its passage with an impetuous embrace. On this mighty tide the black ships—laden with the fresh-scented fir-planks, with rounded sacks of oil-bearing seed, or with the dark glitter of coal—are borne along to the town of St. Ogg's, which shows its aged, fluted red roofs and the broad gables of its wharves between the low wooded hill and the river brink, tinging the water with a soft purple hue under the transient glance of this February sun. Far away on each hand stretch the rich pastures, and the patches of dark earth, made ready for the seed of broad-leaved green crops, or touched already with the tint of the tender-bladed autumn-sown corn. There is a remnant still of the last year's golden clusters of beehive ricks rising at intervals beyond the hedgerows; and everywhere the hedgerows are studded with trees: the distant ships seem to be lifting their masts and stretching their red-brown sails close among the branches of the spreading ash. Just by the red-roofed town the tributary Ripple flows with a lively current into the Floss. How lovely the little river is, with its dark, changing wavelets! It seems to me like a living companion while I wander along the bank and listen to its low placid voice, as to the voice of one who is deaf and loving. I remember those large dipping willows. I remember the stone bridge.

And this is Dorlcote Mill. I must stand a minute or two here on the bridge and look at it, though the clouds are threatening, and it is far on in the afternoon. Even in this leafless time of departing February it is pleasant to look at—perhaps the chill damp season adds a charm to the trimly-kept, comfortable dwelling-house, as old as the elms and chestnuts that shelter it from the northern blast. The stream is brimful now, and lies high in this little withy plantation, and half drowns the grassy fringe of the croft in front of the house. As I look at the full stream, the vivid grass, the delicate bright-green powder softening the outline of the great trunks and branches that gleam from under the bare purple boughs, I am in love with moistness, and envy the white ducks that are dipping their heads far into the water here among the withes, unmindful of the awkward appearance they make in the drier world above.

The rush of the water, and the booming of the mill, bring a dreamy deafness, which seems to heighten the peacefulness of the scene. They are like a great curtain of sound, shutting one out from the world beyond. And now there is the thunder of the huge covered waggon coming home with sacks of grain. That honest waggoner is thinking of his dinner, getting sadly dry in the oven at this late hour; but he will not touch it till he has fed his horses,—the strong, submissive, meek-eyed beasts, who, I fancy, are looking mild reproach at him from between their blinkers, that he should crack his whip at them in that awful manner as if they needed that hint! See how they stretch their shoulders up the slope towards the bridge, with all the more energy because they are so near home. Look at their grand shaggy feet that seem to grasp the firm earth, at the patient strength of their necks, bowed under the heavy collar, at the mighty muscles of their struggling haunches! I should like well to hear

72

them neigh over their hardly-earned feed of corn, and see them, with their moist necks freed from the harness, dipping their eager nostrils into the muddy pond. Now they are on the bridge, and down they go again at a swifter pace, and the arch of the covered waggon disappears at the turning behind the trees.

Now I can turn my eyes towards the mill again, and watch the unresting wheel sending out its diamond jets of water. That little girl is watching it too: she has been standing on just the same spot at the edge of the water ever since I paused on the bridge. And that queer white cur with the brown ear seems to be leaping and barking in ineffectual remonstrance with the wheel; perhaps he is jealous, because his playfellow in the beaver bonnet is so rapt in its movement. It is time the little playfellow went in, I think; and there is a very bright fire to tempt her: the red light shines out under the deepening grey of the sky. It is time, too, for me to leave off resting my arms on the cold stone of this bridge. . . .

Ah, my arms are really benumbed. I have been pressing my elbows on the arms of my chair, and dreaming that I was standing on the bridge in front of Dorlcote Mill, as it looked one February afternoon many years ago. Before I dozed off, I was going to tell you what Mr. and Mrs. Tulliver were talking about, as they sat by the bright fire in the left-hand parlour, on that very afternoon I have been dreaming of.

7. **Which animal is mentioned in the passage?**

    a. Dog
    b. Cat
    c. Rabbit
    d. Ox
    e. Mole

8. **What can we infer about the narrator?**

    a. She is a child.
    b. She worked at the mill.
    c. She is standing on the bridge.
    d. She has fond memories of this place.
    e. She lives here.

9. **In paragraph 2, what device is used to compare the sounds of the mill and the river to a curtain of sound?**

    a. Symbolism
    b. Simile
    c. Personification
    d. Hyperbole
    e. Metaphor

10. **Paragraph 3 makes use of what literary device?**

    a. Foreshadowing
    b. Pun
    c. Oxymoron
    d. Allusion
    e. Contrast

11. Which is described in the excerpt as "dark" and "deaf"?
a. The horses
b. The waggoner
c. The river
d. The stone bridge
e. Dorlcote Mill

12. The narrative technique used in this excerpt is
a. Second person
b. Third-person limited omniscience
c. Unreliable narrator
d. Third person
e. Omniscient narrator

Questions 13-18 pertain to the following passage:

The Bible, Job 38

1: Then the LORD answered Job out of the whirlwind, and said,

2: Who is this that darkeneth counsel by words without knowledge?

3: Gird up now thy loins like a man; for I will demand of thee, and answer thou me.

4: Where wast thou when I laid the foundations of the earth? Declare, if thou hast understanding.

5: Who hath laid the measures thereof, if thou knowest? Or who hath stretched the line upon it?

6: Whereupon are the foundations thereof fastened? Or who laid the corner stone thereof;

7: When the morning stars sang together, and all the sons of God shouted for joy?

8: Or who shut up the sea with doors, when it brake forth, as if it had issued out of the womb?

9: When I made the cloud the garment thereof, and thick darkness a swaddling band for it,

10: And brake up for it my decreed place, and set bars and doors,

11: And said, Hitherto shalt thou come, but no further: and here shall thy proud waves be stayed?

12: Hast thou commanded the morning since thy days; and caused the dayspring to know his place;

13: That it might take hold of the ends of the earth, that the wicked might be shaken out of it?

14: It is turned as clay to the seal; and they stand as a garment.

15: And from the wicked their light is withholden, and the high arm shall be broken.

16: Hast thou entered into the springs of the sea? Or hast thou walked in the search of the depth?

17: Have the gates of death been opened unto thee? Or hast thou seen the doors of the shadow of death?

18: Hast thou perceived the breadth of the earth? Declare if thou knowest it all.

19: Where is the way where light dwelleth? And as for darkness, where is the place thereof,

20: That thou shouldest take it to the bound thereof, and that thou shouldest know the paths to the house thereof?

21: Knowest thou it, because thou wast then born? Or because the number of thy days is great?

22: Hast thou entered into the treasures of the snow? Or hast thou seen the treasures of the hail,

23: Which I have reserved against the time of trouble, against the day of battle and war?

24: By what way is the light parted, which scattereth the east wind upon the earth?

25: Who hath divided a watercourse for the overflowing of waters, or a way for the lightning of thunder;

26: To cause it to rain on the earth, where no man is; on the wilderness, wherein there is no man;

27: To satisfy the desolate and waste ground; and to cause the bud of the tender herb to spring forth?

28: Hath the rain a father? Or who hath begotten the drops of dew?

29: Out of whose womb came the ice? And the hoary frost of heaven, who hath gendered it?

30: The waters are hid as with a stone, and the face of the deep is frozen.

31: Canst thou bind the sweet influences of Pleiades, or loose the bands of Orion?

32: Canst thou bring forth Mazzaroth in his season? Or canst thou guide Arcturus with his sons?

33: Knowest thou the ordinances of heaven? Canst thou set the dominion thereof in the earth?

34: Canst thou lift up thy voice to the clouds, that abundance of waters may cover thee?

35: Canst thou send lightnings, that they may go, and say unto thee, Here we are?

36: Who hath put wisdom in the inward parts? Or who hath given understanding to the heart?

37: Who can number the clouds in wisdom? Or who can stay the bottles of heaven,

38: When the dust groweth into hardness, and the clods cleave fast together?

39: Wilt thou hunt the prey for the lion? Or fill the appetite of the young lions,

40: When they couch in their dens, and abide in the covert to lie in wait?

41: Who provideth for the raven his food? When his young ones cry unto God, they wander for lack of meat.

13. This passage uses

a. Sententia
b. Hyperbole
c. Sarcasm
d. Rhetorical questions
e. Epithet

14. Which overall point is God making in this chapter?

a. I created everything, because I am all-powerful.
b. You are powerless, because you are a human.
c. My creation proves I have greater wisdom than you.
d. The heavens contain many wonders which I created.
e. I am much older than you.

15. This excerpt is written as

a. Prophecy
b. A didactic poem
c. Apocalyptic prose
d. Epistolary prose
e. A narrative essay

16. In verse 6, what does "thereof" refer to?

a. Foundations
b. The seas
c. Creation
d. The morning stars
e. The earth

17. Constellations are discussed in which verse(s)?

a. 31–32
b. 19–20
c. 34–35
d. 24–26
e. 7

18. In verse 12, what is the meaning of "dayspring?"

a. Proud waves
b. Creation
c. Morning stars
d. Dawn
e. The waters

Questions 19-23 pertain to the following passage:

Roughing It, Mark Twain (1872)

This book is merely a personal narrative, and not a pretentious history or a philosophical dissertation. It is a record of several years of variegated vagabondizing, and its object is rather to help the resting reader while away an idle hour than afflict him with metaphysics, or goad him with science. Still, there is information in the volume; information concerning an interesting episode in the history of the Far West, about which no books have been written by persons who were on the ground in person, and saw the happenings of the time with their own eyes. I allude to the rise, growth and culmination of the silver-mining fever in Nevada—a curious episode, in some respects; the only one, of its peculiar kind, that has occurred in the land; and the only one, indeed, that is likely to occur in it.

Yes, take it all around, there is quite a good deal of information in the book. I regret this very much; but really it could not be helped: information appears to stew out of me naturally, like the precious ottar of roses out of the otter. Sometimes it has seemed to me that I would give worlds if I could retain my facts; but it cannot be. The more I calk up the sources, and the tighter I get, the more I leak wisdom. Therefore, I can only claim indulgence at the hands of the reader, not justification.

19. In referring to "variegated vagabondizing" and the "resting reader," Twain makes use of what literary device?

a. Simile
b. Hyperbole
c. Onomatopoeia
d. Alliteration
e. Personification

20. The style of this piece could be termed what?

a. Vernacular
b. Dystopian
c. Liturgical
d. Apologue
e. Allegorical

21. What does the writer mean in the last sentence?

a. I would like to have written a shorter book, but I just have too much information.
b. I hope you'll bear with me in wading through all of the information in this book, although I'm not expecting you to understand why I included it all.
c. I apologize for the amount of history I'm about to present.
d. My readers have been so indulgent with me that I am using their kindness as a reason to wax eloquent in this book.
e. I hope you enjoy this book, but I don't really expect you to.

22. The forthcoming story will not contain much

a. History
b. Eyewitness testimony
c. Geography
d. Humor
e. Science

23. What does Twain regret, in the second sentence of the second paragraph?

a. That there are so few eyewitness accounts of the West's history
b. That he has accrued such wisdom
c. That this book has become a personal narrative
d. That there is so much information in this book
e. That so much wisdom has leaked

Questions 24-29 pertain to the following passage:

Macbeth, William Shakespeare

Tomorrow, and tomorrow, and tomorrow,

Creeps in this petty pace from day to day

To the last syllable of recorded time,

And all our yesterdays have lighted fools

The way to dusty death.

Out, out, brief candle!

Life's but a walking shadow, a poor player

That struts and frets his hour upon the stage

And then is heard no more: it is a tale

Told by an idiot, full of sound and fury,

Signifying nothing.

24. The doctrine evoked by this passage is

a. Solipsism
b. Nihilism
c. Fatalism
d. Fallibilism
e. Determinism

25. The meter of the piece is

a. Iambic trimeter
b. Trochaic meter
c. Anapestic meter
d. Iambic pentameter
e. Pyrrhic meter

26. Who is on the way to dusty death?

a. Fools
b. Yesterday
c. The candle
d. Macbeth
e. The reader

27. Life is compared to all of the following except what?

a. A candle
b. A tale
c. A shadow
d. A stage
e. Tomorrow, and tomorrow, and tomorrow

28. Why is the player "poor?"

a. He is an idiot.
b. He is fretting.
c. His life is meaningless.
d. He can't speak.
e. He is omniscient.

29. The two sections of the passage differ in which way?

a. The first section reads smoothly; the second is choppier.
b. The first section is melancholy; the second is hopeful.
c. The first section is spoken by Macbeth, the second by his wife.
d. The meter changes from the first section to the second.
e. The first section refers to birth, the second to death.

Questions 30-34 pertain to the following passage:

Emma, Jane Austen (1816)

"I have none of the usual inducements of women to marry. Were I to fall in love, indeed, it would be a different thing! but I never have been in love; it is not my way, or my nature; and I do not think I ever shall. And, without love, I am sure I should be a fool to change such a situation as mine.

Fortune I do not want; employment I do not want; consequence I do not want: I believe few married women are half as much mistress of their husband's house, as I am of Hartfield; and never, never could I expect to be so truly beloved and important; so always first and always right in any man's eyes as I am in my father's."

"But then, to be an old maid at last, like Miss Bates!"

"That is as formidable an image as you could present, Harriet; and if I thought I should ever be like Miss Bates! so silly—so satisfied—so smiling—so prosing—so undistinguishing and unfastidious—and so apt to tell every thing relative to every body about me, I would marry tomorrow. But between us, I am convinced there never can be any likeness, except in being unmarried."

"But still, you will be an old maid! and that's so dreadful!"

"Never mind, Harriet, I shall not be a poor old maid; and it is poverty only which makes celibacy contemptible to a generous public! A single woman, with a very narrow income, must be a ridiculous, disagreeable, old maid! the proper sport of boys and girls; but a single woman, of good fortune, is always respectable, and may be as sensible and pleasant as any body else. And the distinction is not quite so much against the candour and common sense of the world as appears at first, for a very narrow income has a tendency to contract the mind, and sour the temper. Those who can barely live, and who live perforce in a very small, and generally very inferior, society, may well be illiberal and cross.

30. What is the point made by the main speaker?
    a. She doesn't plan to become an old maid.
    b. Being single is a liability only if one is poor.
    c. She doesn't like Miss Bates.
    d. She has never been in love.
    e. Being celibate is contemptible to the public.

31. Which does not describe Miss Bates?
    a. Unfastidious
    b. Silly
    c. Unmarried
    d. Beloved
    e. Smiling

32. Identify the primary literary devices used in the following lines: "so silly – so satisfied – so smiling – so prosing – so undistinguishing and unfastidious – and so apt to tell every thing relative to every body about me."
    a. Simile and alliteration
    b. Personification and rhyme
    c. Assonance and consonance
    d. Alliteration and consonance
    e. Consonance and personification

33. In the final line, "illiberal" means what?

a. Poor and destitute
b. Conservative and angry
c. Small and inferior
d. Angry and frustrated
e. Narrow-minded and selfish

34. Which phrase shows alliteration?

a. "I am sure I should be a fool to change such a situation."
b. "A very narrow income has a tendency to contract the mind, and sour the temper."
c. "So always first and always right in any man's eyes as I am in my father's."
d. "I am convinced there never can be any likeness, except in being unmarried."
e. "A single woman, with a very narrow income, must be a ridiculous, disagreeable, old maid!"

Questions 35-39 pertain to the following passage:

Stopping by Woods on a Snowy Evening, Robert Frost (1923)

Whose woods these are I think I know.
His house is in the village though;
He will not see me stopping here
To watch his woods fill up with snow.

My little horse must think it queer
To stop without a farmhouse near
Between the woods and frozen lake
The darkest evening of the year.

He gives his harness bells a shake
To ask if there is some mistake.
The only other sound's the sweep
Of easy wind and downy flake.

The woods are lovely, dark and deep.
But I have promises to keep,
And miles to go before I sleep,
And miles to go before I sleep.

35. The rhyme scheme of most of the stanzas is

a. abaa
b. abab
c. aaaa
d. abcc
e. aaba

36. What is the meter used in this poem?

a. Iambic pentameter
b. Iambic tetrameter
c. Accentual meter
d. Anapestic
e. Trochaic

37. **"He gives his harness bells a shake**

To ask if there is some mistake" (third stanza) is an example of what?

 a. Personification

 b. Simile

 c. Alliteration

 d. Assonance

 e. Hyperbole

38. From the first four lines, what can we infer about the woods' owner?

 a. He and the author are close friends.

 b. The author works for him.

 c. The author is his relative.

 d. He is watching.

 e. The author is envious of him.

39. Why might the final line of the poem be repeated?

 a. Because "sleep" rhymes with "keep" and "deep"

 b. To emphasize the monotony of the long journey

 c. To simulate the sound of the horse

 d. To create four lines in the stanza

 e. Because the speaker is falling asleep

Questions 40-44 pertain to the following passage:

The Pit and the Pendulum, Edgar Allan Poe (1843)

I WAS sick, sick unto death, with that long agony, and when they at length unbound me, and I was permitted to sit, I felt that my senses were leaving me. The sentence, the dread sentence of death, was the last of distinct accentuation which reached my ears. After that, the sound of the inquisitorial voices seemed merged in one dreamy indeterminate hum. It conveyed to my soul the idea of REVOLUTION, perhaps from its association in fancy with the burr of a mill-wheel. This only for a brief period, for presently I heard no more. Yet, for a while, I saw, but with how terrible an exaggeration! I saw the lips of the black-robed judges. They appeared to me white— whiter than the sheet upon which I trace these words—and thin even to grotesqueness; thin with the intensity of their expression of firmness, of immovable resolution, of stern contempt of human torture. I saw that the decrees of what to me was fate were still issuing from those lips. I saw them writhe with a deadly locution. I saw them fashion the syllables of my name, and I shuddered, because no sound succeeded. I saw, too, for a few moments of delirious horror, the soft and nearly imperceptible waving of the sable draperies which enwrapped the walls of the apartment; and then my vision fell upon the seven tall candles upon the table. At first they wore the aspect of charity, and seemed white slender angels who would save me: but then all at once there came a most deadly nausea over my spirit, and I felt every fibre in my frame thrill, as if I had touched the wire of a galvanic battery, while the angel forms became meaningless spectres, with heads of flame, and I saw that from them there would be no help. And then there stole into my fancy, like a rich musical note, the thought of what sweet rest there must be in the grave. The thought came gently and stealthily, and it seemed long before it attained full appreciation; but just as my spirit came at length properly to feel and entertain it, the figures of the judges vanished, as if magically, from before me; the tall candles sank into nothingness; their flames went out utterly; the blackness of darkness superened; all sensations appeared swallowed up in a mad rushing descent as of the soul into Hades. Then silence, and stillness, and night were the universe.

I had swooned; but still will not say that all of consciousness was lost. What of it there remained I will not attempt to define, or even to describe; yet all was not lost. In the deepest slumber—no! In delirium—no! In a swoon—no! In death—no! Even in the grave all was not lost. Else there is no immortality for man. Arousing from the most profound of slumbers, we break the gossamer web of some dream. Yet in a second afterwards (so frail may that web have been) we remember not that we have dreamed. In the return to life from the swoon there are two stages; first, that of the sense of mental or spiritual; secondly, that of the sense of physical existence. It seems probable that if, upon reaching the second stage, we could recall the impressions of the first, we should find these impressions eloquent in memories of the gulf beyond. And that gulf is, what? How at least shall we distinguish its shadows from those of the tomb? But if the impressions of what I have termed the first stage are not at will recalled, yet, after long interval, do they not come unbidden, while we marvel whence they come? He who has never swooned is not he who finds strange palaces and wildly familiar faces in coals that glow; is not he who beholds floating in mid-air the sad visions that the many may not view; is not he who ponders over the perfume of some novel flower; is not he whose brain grows bewildered with the meaning of some musical cadence which has never before arrested his attention.

40. The selection is written in

a. First-person narration
b. Third-person narration
c. First-person omniscient narration
d. Epistolary narrative voice
e. Second-person narration

41. A key concept of the second paragraph is that

a. We all dream.
b. The legal system can result in injustice.
c. Dreams are a part of sleeping.
d. There is awareness even in unconsciousness.
e. Death can offer rest.

42. What is compared to white slender angels?

a. The sable draperies
b. The judges' lips
c. Seven tall candles
d. Rich musical notes
e. Silence and stillness

43. This descriptive passage contains many examples of

a. Trochaic pentameter
b. Alliteration
c. Soraismus
d. Assonance
e. Enargia

44. The main emotion the narrator expresses is

a. Ambivalence
b. Annoyance
c. Horror
d. Uncertainty
e. Hope

Questions 45-50 pertain to the following passage:

A Doll's House, Henrik Ibsen (1879)

Nora. It is true. I have loved you above everything else in the world.

Helmer. Oh, don't let us have any silly excuses.

Nora [taking a step towards him]. Torvald—!

Helmer. Miserable creature—what have you done?

Nora. Let me go. You shall not suffer for my sake. You shall not take it upon yourself.

Helmer. No tragic airs, please. [Locks the hall door.] Here you shall stay and give me an explanation. Do you understand what you have done? Answer me! Do you understand what you have done?

Nora [looks steadily at him and says with a growing look of coldness in her face]. Yes, now I am beginning to understand thoroughly.

Helmer [walking about the room]. What a horrible awakening! All these eight years—she who was my joy and pride—a hypocrite, a liar—worse, worse—a criminal! The unutterable ugliness of it all!—For shame! For shame! [NORA is silent and looks steadily at him. He stops in front of her.] I ought to have suspected that something of the sort would happen. I ought to have foreseen it. All your father's want of principle—be silent!—all your father's want of principle has come out in you. No religion, no morality, no sense of duty—. How I am punished for having winked at what he did! I did it for your sake, and this is how you repay me.

Nora. Yes, that's just it.

Helmer. Now you have destroyed all my happiness. You have ruined all my future. It is horrible to think of! I am in the power of an unscrupulous man; he can do what he likes with me, ask anything he likes of me, give me any orders he pleases—I dare not refuse. And I must sink to such miserable depths because of a thoughtless woman!

Nora. When I am out of the way, you will be free.

Helmer. No fine speeches, please. Your father had always plenty of those ready, too. What good would it be to me if you were out of the way, as you say? Not the slightest. He can make the affair known everywhere; and if he does, I may be falsely suspected of having been a party to your criminal action. Very likely people will think I was behind it all—that it was I who prompted you! And I have to thank you for all this—you whom I have cherished during the whole of our married life. Do you understand now what it is you have done for me?

84

Nora [coldly and quietly]. Yes.

Helmer. It is so incredible that I can't take it in. But we must come to some understanding. Take off that shawl. Take it off, I tell you. I must try and appease him some way or another. The matter must be hushed up at any cost. And as for you and me, it must appear as if everything between us were just as before—but naturally only in the eyes of the world. You will still remain in my house, that is a matter of course. But I shall not allow you to bring up the children; I dare not trust them to you. To think that I should be obliged to say so to one whom I have loved so dearly, and whom I still—. No, that is all over. From this moment happiness is not the question; all that concerns us is to save the remains, the fragments, the appearance—

[A ring is heard at the front-door bell.]

Helmer [with a start]. What is that? So late! Can the worst—? Can he—? Hide yourself, Nora. Say you are ill.

****

Helmer (Standing at Nora's doorway.) Try and calm yourself, and make your mind easy again, my frightened little singing-bird. Be at rest, and feel secure; I have broad wings to shelter you under. (Walks up and down by the door.) How warm and cozy our home is, Nora. Here is shelter for you; here I will protect you like a hunted dove that I have saved from a hawk's claws; I will bring peace to your poor beating heart. It will come, little by little, Nora, believe me. Tomorrow morning you will look upon it all quite differently; soon everything will be just as it was before.

Very soon you won't need me to assure you that I have forgiven you; you will yourself feel the certainty that I have done so. Can you suppose I should ever think of such a thing as repudiating you, or even reproaching you? You have no idea what a true man's heart is like, Nora. There is something so indescribably sweet and satisfying, to a man, in the knowledge that he has forgiven his wife—forgiven her freely, and with all his heart. It seems as if that had made her, as it were, doubly his own; he has given her a new life, so to speak; and she is in a way become both wife and child to him.

So you shall be for me after this, my little scared, helpless darling. Have no anxiety about anything, Nora; only be frank and open with me, and I will serve as will and conscience both to you—. What is this? Not gone to bed? Have you changed your things?

45. What can we infer about Nora's father?
a. He was not a good speaker.
b. He was a fisherman.
c. He was lacking in morals.
d. He can make the affair known.
e. He rings the doorbell.

46. Helmer's words to Nora are full of

a. Contradictions
b. Praise
c. Explanation
d. Hyperbole
e. None of the above

47. In Helmer's final monologues, why does he describe Nora as "little?"

a. Because she is afraid of him
b. Because she is much younger than he
c. Because she is very petite
d. To emphasize her relative size
e. To emphasize his dominance

48. What are the main qualities Helmer conveys in his final monologue?

a. Love and forgiveness
b. Pity and affection
c. Pride and humility
d. Anger and passion
e. Bravado and condescension

49. What can we infer about the relationship between Nora and Helmer?

I. Nora tries to control Helmer.
II. Helmer sees himself as superior to Nora.
III. They see themselves as equals.

a. I only
b. II only
c. III only
d. I and II
e. I and III

50. Helmer makes use of which symbol?

a. Hypocrite
b. Their home
c. Criminal
d. Birds
e. Children

Questions 51 – 56 pertain to the following passage:

Percy Bysshe Shelley, "Ozymandias"

I met a traveller from an antique land
Who said: "Two vast and trunkless legs of stone
Stand in the desert. Near them on the sand,
Half sunk, a shattered visage lies, whose frown
And wrinkled lip and sneer of cold command
Tell that its sculptor well those passions read
Which yet survive, stamped on these lifeless things,
The hand that mocked them and the heart that fed.

And on the pedestal these words appear:
`My name is Ozymandias, King of Kings:
Look on my works, ye mighty, and despair!'
Nothing beside remains. Round the decay
Of that colossal wreck, boundless and bare,
The lone and level sands stretch far away."

51. What is the rhyme scheme of the first eight lines?

a. ABACADAC
b. ABABACDC
c. ABABABCB
d. ABADACDC
e. ABABCBCB

52. What is the central image of the poem?

a. A collapsed statue in the desert
b. A wounded king
c. A face and inscription on a coin
d. A plaque near a WWII battle site
e. The Sphinx

53. In what sense are lines 10-11 ironic? Although the inscription was originally intended to boast of a king's power, it appears to later generations as an example of how:

a. Engineering skills were not as advanced as people believed at the time
b. A king's power extends only as far as the boundaries of his kingdom
c. A king can attain immortality through his works
d. Time and nature will eventually undo the works of even the mighty
e. The desert is not a suitable climate for a kingdom

54. Read as a symbol, the desert can be seen to represent:

a. Fertility
b. The life cycle
c. The seasons
d. Life
e. A wasteland

55. Based on the setting, which of the following do you think best describes Ozymandias?

a. Roman Emperor
b. Egyptian Pharaoh
c. Native American Chief
d. Dynastic Emperor
e. English Monarch

56. What poetic form does this poem use?

a. Italian sonnet
b. Ballad
c. Anaphora
d. Prose poem
e. Sestina

Questions 57 – 60 pertain to the following passage:

Emily Dickinson, "Success is counted sweetest"

Success is counted sweetest
By those who ne'er succeed.
To comprehend a nectar
Requires sorest need.

Not one of all the purple Host
Who took the Flag today
Can tell the definition
So clear of Victory

As he defeated--dying--
On whose forbidden ear
The distant strains of triumph
Burst agonized and clear!

57. In the final stanza, the imagery suggests a soldier who lies dying on a battlefield. Which of the following interpretations of lines from the poem reinforce this image?

> I. The final line suggests cannon blasts
> II. "Strains of triumph" imply the dying soldier's joy in victory
> III. The words "defeated, dying" in line 9 indicate mortal combat

a. I only
b. I and II
c. II and III
d. I and III
e. II only

58. What literary device is employed in lines 3 and 4?

a. Paradox
b. Caesura
c. Metaphor
d. Dramatic monologue
e. Anaphora

59. How many stressed syllables are in each line of the first stanza?

a. 1
b. 2
c. 3
d. 4
e. 5

60. By what logical pattern is this poem organized?

a. Main idea, developed with examples
b. Cause and effect
c. Comparison and contrast
d. Chronological order
e. Description

88

Answers and Explanations 1

1. D: The entire poem is a metaphor for the journey of life. We are born and hope for a long life, meet with obstacles, hope for the best, and enjoy our experiences along the way.

The Middle East is too specific to be a metaphor in the poem.

The poem describes an experience broader and more long-range than young love, adolescence, or a battle.

2. B: Several mentions are made of characters from Homer's *The Odyssey*. Among them are the Lestrygonians, the Cyclops, and angry Poseidon, all enemies of Odysseus. Ithaca itself was inspired by Odysseus' island kingdom.

3. E: The voyage to Ithaca is symbolic of our life's journey. The journey is what we should savor, but at the same time we shouldn't expect too much from the destination. Our starting and ending points are not as important as the journey.

4. A: The poem is written in second-person imperative, meaning it is addressed to the reader ("you"), and is instructing the reader what to do. Second-person imperative is rarely seen in narrative works, but it can be effective in poetic works such as this.

5. C: This stanza refers to stopping at ports in Phoenician markets to buy fine things and perfumes. This is advising the reader to enjoy the fine things in life when they are available. The Egyptian cities mentioned symbolize knowledge and education, and the reader is urged to visit these ports (not once, but throughout life) and to take advantage of their offerings.

6. D: "Her" in this case refers to Ithaca, the beginning and ending point of the journey detailed in the poem. The desire to return to Ithaca has inspired the journey and has led to all of its beauty and challenges.

7. A: "... that queer white cur with the brown ear" in paragraph 4 refers to a dog. A cur is a mixed-breed dog.

8. D: The passage implies that the narrator has fond memories of this place. She describes the "loving tide," "rich pastures," and the "honest waggoner." She tells us "how lovely the little river is," and "I remember the stone bridge."

We can assume she is not a child, as she recalls the mill "many years ago." Although she may have worked at the mill, that is not specifically implied. She tells us she is in her chair, "dreaming that I was standing on the bridge." She may live here or may not, but we cannot tell from this passage.

9. B: "The rush of the water, and the booming of the mill, bring a dreamy deafness, which seems to heighten the peacefulness of the scene. They are like a great curtain of sound, shutting one out from the world beyond."

The rush of water and the booming of the mills are like a great curtain of sound. Comparisons using like or as are known as similes.

89

10. E: Paragraph 3 is marked by contrast: the loud sounds of the mill contrasting with the peacefulness of the scene, the thunder of the wagon contrasted with the meek-eyed horses, who are strong yet submissive.

11. C: The river is referred to in paragraph 1 as "... lovely ... with its dark, changing wavelets! It seems to me like a living companion while I wander along the bank and listen to its low placid voice, as to the voice of one who is deaf and loving." Contrast is used again as the river is described both favorably and unfavorably.

12. E: The passage features an omniscient narrator writing in the first-person. This means that she knows everything about the places and characters in the story (i.e., she is omniscient), although all of this information is not revealed at the outset.

13. D: This chapter is noted for its rhetorical questions: questions that do not necessarily require an answer, although they often imply an answer. Rhetorical questions are often used in debate to avoid making a declaration plainly, but to make a point nonetheless.

14. C: Although each of the answers could be argued, the overriding point of the chapter is "My creation proves I have greater wisdom than you." Verses 4–41 detail various elements of God's creation, and his questions asking whether Job knows the details of these things imply "no" answers. Verse 3: "Gird up now thy loins like a man; for I will demand of thee, and answer thou me" implies that God sees himself as possessing greater wisdom in this situation.

15. B: Job is written as a didactic poem set in a prose frame: a lyrical writing style that teaches a moral lesson. In the case of Job, the book explores the issue of why God allows good people to suffer.

16. E: "Thereof" refers to the earth, mentioned in verse 4: "Where wast thou when I laid the foundations of the earth?" Verses 5 and 6 continue to refer to the earth and its creation.

17. A: Verses 31–32 mention several constellations: Pleiades, also known as the Seven Sisters constellation; Orion, known as the hunter; Mazzaroth, which refers to Zodiac constellations; and Arcturus, the brightest star in the constellation Bootes.

18. D: "Hast thou commanded the morning since thy days; and caused the dayspring to know his place"

Dayspring refers to the dawn; the "place" of the dayspring being the spot on the horizon where the sun appears to rise. This meaning is consistent with the discussion of morning in the first part of the verse.

19. D: Alliteration is used here, since both words begin with "v" in the first example and "r" in the second. Simile compares two objects, while hyperbole is a device in which language is deliberately exaggerated. Onomatopoeia is the use of language which sounds like what it is (examples: buzz, gong, crackle). Personification is the giving of human traits to inanimate objects.

20. A: This piece (along with much of Twain's work) is written in a style called the vernacular, in which the writer writes as he would speak, using native or everyday language. The vernacular contrasts with more literary forms of writing.

21. B: Therefore, I can only claim indulgence at the hands of the reader, not justification.

In the first phrase, Twain asks his readers for indulgence, or for patience and perseverance in continuing on with him. He doesn't request justification, which refers to his talk in previous sentences about his vast amounts of knowledge. He isn't asking the reader's permission to tell all of his stories.

22. E: Twain says that his object is "rather to help the resting reader while away an idle hour than afflict him with metaphysics, or goad him with science."

So, while we may not expect much science from the book, we are told that it is an eyewitness account of several events not much noted in history. Twain will recount his adventures traveling in the Far West, which will no doubt include geography. Twain's style of writing involves much dry humor.

23. D: "I regret this very much" refers back to the previous sentence, in which Twain has told us that the book will contain much information. Here, Twain tells us that he regrets "this" (surplus of information) very much, in an example of his trademark dry humor.

24. B: The passage illustrates nihilism, the belief that life is meaningless and without purpose or intrinsic value. It evokes a feeling of despair at the perceived pointlessness of existence.

Solipsism is the belief that one's own mind is all that exists.

Fatalism assigns all of life's events to fate.

Fallibilism contends that all human knowledge could be mistaken (some contend that certainty about any knowledge is impossible).

Determinism states that every human event is causally determined by a chain of prior events.

25. D: The piece is written in iambic pentameter. Iambic refers to a pattern of an unaccented syllable followed by an accented syllable (one set of this pattern is called a foot). Pentameter means that there are five consecutive feet (i.e., da DUM, da DUM, da DUM, da DUM, da DUM).

26. A: "And all our yesterdays have lighted fools

The way to dusty death"

"For" is implied between lighted and fools. Shakespeare omitted it to preserve the meter of the line and because it is implied that "fools" is an indirect object.

27. D: The stage is presented as a venue where life is lived. "Tomorrow, and tomorrow, and tomorrow," a candle, a tale, and a shadow are compared to life in the excerpt.

28. C: Shakespeare's reference to the "poor player" on stage for his brief time illustrates the passage's overall nihilistic tone: life is meaningless, so pity the poor mortals who are living.

29. A: The first section consists of multi-syllable words, soft consonants and vowels. The second section consists of more one-syllable words and hard consonants, perhaps indicating an evolution in thought by Macbeth as he speaks the passage (the entire passage is spoken by Macbeth in response to learning of his wife's death).

30. B: The speaker (Emma) uses this passage to convey her opinion that being single is only a hardship if one is poor. Her first paragraph iterates the reasons she has for being happy with her

current situation, and she then says "it is poverty only which makes celibacy contemptible to a generous public." She further states that "a very narrow income" can "contract the mind and sour the temper."

31. D: Emma uses unfastidious, silly, unmarried, and smiling all to describe Miss Bates. Emma describes herself as "truly beloved and important."

32. D: Alliteration, or the repetition of initial consonant sounds in close proximity, is used here, as evidenced by the frequent use of "s" sounds. Consonance (repetition of consonant sounds within nearby words) is also used.

33. E: "Illiberal" during Jane Austen's day meant narrow-minded, selfish, and ungenerous. This is implied in the passage: "Those who

can barely live, and who live perforce in a very small, and generally very inferior, society, may well be illiberal and cross."

If one barely lives in a small, inferior society, this leads to having a narrow frame of reference and (perhaps of necessity) being selfish.

34. A: Alliteration, or the repetition of initial consonant sounds in words of close proximity, is shown in the words sure, should, such, and situation.

35. E: The rhyme scheme for the first three stanzas is aaba (in stanza one, "know," "though," and "snow" rhyme and form *a*; "here" is *b*.

The final stanza uses aaaa as a rhyme scheme.

36. B: The poem is written in iambic tetrameter, meaning it has four groups (or feet) of two syllables per line. Iambic refers to the two-syllable groups consisting of a first syllable that is unaccented and a second syllable that is accented.

Iambic pentameter consists of five groups of two syllables per line.

Accentual meter is used in Old English poetry and features four stresses per line without attention to unstressed syllables.

Anapestic meter consists of a foot with two unaccented syllables followed by an accented syllable.

Trochaic meter is the opposite of iambic meter: an accented syllable is followed by one that is unaccented.

37. A: The lines are an example of personification, in which a non-human (the horse) is given human qualities (asking a question).

A simile compares two dissimilar things using the words "like" or "as if."

Alliteration is the practice of repeating initial consonants in nearby words.

Assonance is the repetition of the same vowel sound within words.

Hyperbole is intentional exaggeration.

38. E: We can imply that the author is envious of the owner of the woods; his house is in the village (implying wealth), he will not see the author (he is too busy), and the author mentions "his" woods (again, perhaps denoting envy).

39. B: The repetition of "And miles to go before I sleep" emphasizes the tedium of a long journey with a horse. It also helps the poem wind down and fade away, as the rider and his horse slowly fade from view.

40. A: The excerpt is written in first-person narration, meaning that the narrator is a character in the story, telling the story as he ("I") sees it. The narrator is not, however, omniscient, as there are many things about the situation that he does not know.

41. D: The second paragraph illustrates a familiar Poe theme: sleeping, fainting, and even death involve something still living, aware, and acting: "Even in the grave all was not lost." The paragraph ends with a description of the phenomenon known as déjà vu.

42. C: "... my vision fell upon the seven tall candles upon the table. At first, they wore the aspect of charity, and seemed white slender angels who would save me." Poe compares the tall candles to slender white angels at first, but then is horrified to see them seem to transform into "meaningless spectres" that offered no hope.

43. E: Poe's writing is full of enargia, or vivid descriptions. The paragraphs here use vivid language to help the reader feel he is there with the narrator.

An example is the description of the judges' lips: "I saw the lips of the black-robed judges. They appeared to me white—whiter than the sheet upon which I trace these words—and thin even to grotesqueness; thin with the intensity of their expression of firmness, of immovable resolution, of stern contempt of human torture. I saw that the decrees of what to me was fate were still issuing from those lips. I saw them writhe with a deadly locution. I saw them fashion the syllables of my name, and I shuddered, because no sound succeeded."

44. C: The passage overwhelmingly expresses the horror experienced by the narrator ("I WAS sick, sick unto death, with that long agony") as he waits to learn his fate. The passage suggests uncertainty as well, but predominantly the horror and terror the narrator is feeling, as expressed in the language (grotesqueness, terrible, meaningless).

45. C: Helmer's words "all your father's want of principle has come out in you. No religion, no morality, no sense of duty" imply that he feels Nora is exhibiting a lack of morals first exhibited by her father.

46. A: Helmer's words are marked by their contradictions: Nora is his pride and joy, yet a hypocrite and criminal. He loves her dearly, yet will not allow her to bring up the children.

47. E: Helmer uses this monologue to emphasize his dominance over Nora. One way he establishes this is to refer to her twice as "little"—"my frightened little singing bird" and "my little scared, helpless darling."

48. E: Helmer displays his bravado, or swaggering courage, by mentioning his "broad wings" to shelter Nora, as well as how he will protect her and bring her peace. He goes on to speak in a condescending way to her, showing that he perceives her as inferior: "You have no idea what a true man's heart is like" and "I will serve as will and conscience both to you."

49. B: Various passages suggest that Helmer sees himself as superior to Nora; he suggests that he will protect her and be her "will and conscience." He also reprimands her for her lack of religion, morality, and sense of duty, while contrasting this with the way he has "cherished" her all through their married life.

50. D: Helmer uses birds symbolically in his final monologue: he calls Nora his singing bird, tells her that he will shelter her under his broad wings, and tells her that he will protect her like a hunter dove. Although he refers to the other items listed as well, he does not use them as symbols.

51. B: The rhyme scheme of the first eight lines falls into the following pattern: ABABACDC. The rhyming words are, "land," "stone," "sand," "frown," "command," "read," "things," and "fed."

52. A: A collapsed statue in the desert. The image is explicitly described in lines 2 through 4: "Two vast and trunkless legs of stone / Stand in the desert. Near them on the sand, / Half sunk, a shattered visage lies." None of the other choices reflect the imagery of the poem.

53. D: Is the best interpretation of the ironic meaning of the inscription. Irony is used to describe statements or events with multiple levels of meaning. Specifically, it is defined as a statement in which the apparent meaning of the words contradicts the intended meaning. In this case, the poem describes a collapsed statue with an inscription that reads, "Look upon my works, ye mighty, and despair." The original intended meaning of the words was that one should look upon the majesty of Ozymandias's kingdom and despair because of his power. When read underneath a ruined statue, however, the words take on a different apparent meaning, namely that the reader should look at the kingdom and despair because of the destructive forces of time and nature.

54: E: The symbolic meaning of the desert is best read as a wasteland. A symbol is a specific image in a poem that brings to mind some idea or concept that relates back to the poem's themes. Choice (A), fertility, is not likely since a desert rarely calls fertility to mind. Choice (B), the life cycle, is likewise not commonly associated with the desert. Choice (C), the seasons, does not relate to the poem in any meaningful way. Choice (D), life, is so broad that it could be applied to any symbol and does not yield much insight into the themes of this particular poem. Choice (E), a wasteland, is a connotation (or associated meaning) of the desert that does relate back to the theme of the poem, which has to do with the destructive forces of time and the comparative powerlessness of humans.

55. B: An Egyptian Pharaoh, is the best answer because of the poem's setting among ruins in the desert. Choice (A), a Roman Emperor, may be suggested by collapsed statues, but not by the desert landscape. The desert landscape would not refer to choices (C), (D), or (E)—leaders of Native American, Chinese, or English cultures.

56. A: The poem has fourteen lines, which makes the poem a sonnet. Choice (B), ballad, refers to a type of poem with four-line stanzas and iambic meter. Choice (C), anaphora, is a way of creating emphasis by repeating words at the beginning of each line. Choice (D), prose poem, is a more recent form of poetry that does not have line breaks and resembles paragraphs of prose. Choice (E), sestina, refers to a poem with six-line stanzas in which each line ends with one of the same six words.

57. D: The question provides you with an interpretation of the poem. Your job is to identify any of the following statements that help support or prove that interpretation. Choice (D), interpretations I and III, is the best choice. Interpretation II suggests that the dying soldier was victorious in battle, but line nine, "as he defeated, dying" contradicts this reading. Interpretations I and II both reinforce the reading of the stanza as a scene from a battle.

58: C: A metaphor is an implied comparison between two things. In the first stanza, Dickinson creates an implicit comparison between success and nectar (the sweet fluid produced by plants); since she does not use "like" or "as," this type of comparison is called a metaphor, as opposed to a simile, which does. Choice (A), paradox, which means the poem contains contradictory ideas, may be true of the poem as a whole, but metaphor is the best choice for the specific lines three and four because of the implied comparison Dickinson draws between success and nectar. Choice (B), caesura, refers to a pause within the line, but these lines read without pause. Choice (D), dramatic monologue, is a poetic form written in first person in which the speaker is a character in the poem; however, the speaker of Dickinson's poem does not act as a character in the poem. Choice (E), anaphora, is a rhetorical device using repetition, and this poem does not rely heavily on repetition.

59. C: 3 beats per line, is the best answer. With the syllables stressed, the first stanza reads:

SucCESS is COUNted SWEEtest
By THOSE who NE'ER sucCEED.
To COMPreHEND a NECTar
ReQUIres SORest NEED.

Note that there are three stressed syllables per line. The poem varies this structure in the second stanza, adding a fourth stressed syllable in the first line, but for the most part, Dickinson's poem is written in iambic trimeter. "Iambic" refers to a pattern of syllables in which every other syllable is stressed. "Trimeter" means there are three beats per line.

60. A: Dickinson states the main argument of the poem in the first line and provides examples in the form of metaphors to develop that idea. Choice (B), cause and effect, is not the main logical organization of the poem, as this method usually involves isolating a main cause and explaining the effects that result from it. Choice (C), comparison and contrast, most often involves pointing out the similarities and differences between two things, which this poem does not do at length. Choice (D), chronological order, involves describing an event from its first to last moments. Dickinson's poem focuses on multiple events and does not tell which happened first or last. Choice (E), description, usually examines the details of a single item or event; this poem, however, does not provide a great deal of detail for detail's sake.

SAT Practice Test 2

1. Which of the following pieces of literature contains a dramatic irony that is central to the plot?

    a. Walden
    b. A Doll's House
    c. The Three Musketeers
    d. Oedipus Rex
    e. The House of Mirth

2. Which Southern author is known for an astonishing number of grotesque characters?

    a. William Faulkner
    b. John Steinbeck
    c. Eudora Welty
    d. Tennessee Williams
    e. Flannery O'Conner

Questions 3–5 pertain to the following poem:

SONNET 18

> Shall I compare thee to a Summer's day?
> Thou art more lovely and more temperate:
> Rough winds do shake the darling buds of May,
> And Summer's lease hath all too short a date:
> Sometime too hot the eye of heaven shines,
> And oft' is his gold complexion dimm'd;
> And every fair from fair sometime declines,
> By chance or nature's changing course untrimm'd:
> But thy eternal Summer shall not fade
> Nor lose possession of that fair thou owest;
> Nor shall Death brag thou wanderest in his shade,
> When in eternal lines to time thou growest:
> So long as men can breathe, or eyes can see,
> So long lives this, and this gives life to thee.

3. In this Shakespearean sonnet, what is the rhythmic scheme?

    a. Iambic hexameter
    b. Trochee
    c. Anapest
    d. Dactyl
    e. Iambic pentameter

4. To whom is Shakespeare's Sonnet 18 addressed?

    a. A young woman he admires from afar
    b. A married woman with whom he is having an affair
    c. A young man whose beauty he finds divine
    d. A young man with whom he is in love
    e. Himself

5. The third quatrain [beginning at (1)] and the envoy suggest that the youth's beauty will somehow escape time's inevitable destruction. Which of the marked lines—(1), (2), (3), or (4)—offers a play on words that explains how time's ravages will be avoided?

   a. (1)
   b. (2)
   c. (3)
   d. (4)
   e. All the above

6. This 14ᵗʰ century epic poem is a parable of a Christian hereafter from a medieval perspective. Its three sections represent Hell, Purgatory, and Heaven. The name of this Italian masterpiece is:

   a. The Inferno
   b. The Divine Comedy
   c. Remembrance of Things Past
   d. Things Fall Apart
   e. Allegro

7. How is Sethe's attempted murder of her own children in Toni Morrison's famous novel justified?

   a. She doesn't really want to murder them, so she double-crosses herself.
   b. They are the progeny of a man who has been sent by the Devil; there is no hope of their salvation.
   c. She is trying to save them from slavery.
   d. She intends to kill herself as well and to join them on the Other Side.
   e. There is no attempt at justification; the novel is about how evil pervades even the simplest of homes.

8. Virginia Woolf's *Mrs. Dalloway* takes place:

   a. In St. Louis
   b. Days before the end of WWI
   c. Over the course of a day
   d. All the above
   e. None of the above

9. Currently, two viewpoints concerning the original authorship of *Beowulf* stand in opposition to one another. One position states that *Beowulf* was originally _____, the other that it was written by _____.

   a. A children's fairytale with ancient roots; an 18th century podiatrist
   b. Oral tradition; a monk
   c. A folksong; a former warlord turned artist
   d. An annual village play; a hired scribe from another village
   e. An epic poem; a woman who dressed as a man and wore a false beard

Questions 10-12 pertain to the following passage:

Our village life would stagnate if it were not for the unexplored forests and meadows which surround it. We need the tonic of wildness, -- to wade sometimes in marshes where the bittern and the meadow-hen lurk, and hear the booming of the snipe; to smell the whispering sedge where only some wilder and more solitary fowl builds her nest, and the mink crawls with its belly close to the ground. At the same time that we are earnest to explore and learn all things, we require that all things be mysterious and unexplorable, that land and sea be infinitely wild, unsurveyed and unfathomed by us because unfathomable. We can never have enough of Nature. (1) We must be refreshed by the sight of inexhaustible vigor, vast and titanic features, the sea-coast with its wrecks, the wilderness with its living and its decaying trees, the thunder-cloud, and the rain which lasts three weeks and produces freshets. We need to witness our own limits transgressed, and some life pasturing freely where we never wander. We are cheered when we observe the vulture feeding on the carrion which disgusts and disheartens us, and deriving health and strength from the repast. There was a dead horse in the hollow by the path to my house, which compelled me sometimes to go out of my way, especially in the night when the air was heavy, but the assurance it gave me of the strong appetite and inviolable health of Nature was my compensation for this. I love to see that Nature is so rife with life that myriads can be afforded to be sacrificed and suffered to prey on one another; that tender organizations can be so serenely squashed out of existence like pulp, -- tadpoles which herons gobble up, and tortoises and toads run over in the road; and that sometimes it has rained flesh and blood! With the liability to accident, we must see how little account is to be made of it. The impression made on a wise man is that of (2) universal innocence. Poison is not poisonous after all, nor are any wounds fatal. Compassion is a very untenable ground. It must be expeditious. Its pleadings will not bear to be stereotyped.

10. This essay is written by:

    a. Ralph Waldo Emerson

    b. George Bernard Shaw

    c. Henry David Thoreau

    d. E.M. Forester

    e. Virginia Woolf

11. Why does the author write "We can never have enough of Nature"? (1) What does he or she believe by saying this?

    a. It is indescribably beautiful and reminds us we are God's creations.

    b. It is disappearing at a rapid pace, and we must appreciate it while we can.

    c. Nature provides us with materials with which we construct our lives.

    d. Because we are human, we cannot help but celebrate destruction.

    e. We realize that life continues, unlimited by obstacles.

12. "Universal innocence" (2) is a metaphor for:

    a. Original sin

    b. The garden of earthly delights

    c. The unmoral nature of Nature

    d. Universal guilt

    e. The innocence of babes

13. What did the poet W.C. Williams object to in the poetry of Ezra Pound and T.S. Eliot?

    a. Their use of blank verse

    b. Their references to classical works of art and foreign languages

    c. Their heightened use of imagery

    d. Their thinly veiled political positions

    e. Their incorporation of slang and "low language"

14. In *Gulliver's Travels*, Lilliputians, Brobdingnagians, Laputans, and Houyhnhnms are used as:

   a. Symbols
   b. Similes
   c. Hyperbole
   d. Idioms
   e. Clichés

15. Which character in Arthur Miller's play *The Crucible*, claimed she had danced for the Devil but now wanted to experience God's light and called out several other characters as proof?

   a. Ann Putnam
   b. Elizabeth Proctor
   c. John Proctor
   d. Beverly Nurse
   e. Abigail Williams.

Use the following poem to answer question 16:

I saw my soul at rest upon a day
As a bird sleeping in the nest of night,

Among soft leaves that give the starlight way
To touch its wings but not its eyes with light;

So that it knew as one in visions may,
And knew not as men waking, of delight.

This was the measure of my soul's delight;
It had no power of joy to fly by day,

Nor part in the large lordship of the light;
But in a secret moon-beholden way

Had all its will of dreams and pleasant night,
And all the love and life that sleepers may.

But such life's triumph as men waking may
It might not have to feed its faint delight

Between the stars by night and sun by day,
Shut up with green leaves and a little light;

Because its way was as a lost star's way,
A world's not wholly known of day or night.

All loves and dreams and sounds and gleams of night
Made it all music that such minstrels may,

And all they had they gave it of delight;
But in the full face of the fire of day

What place shall be for any starry light,
What part of heaven in all the wide sun's way?

Yet the soul woke not, sleeping by the way,
Watched as a nursling of the large-eyed night,

And sought no strength nor knowledge of the day,
Nor closer touch conclusive of delight,

Nor mightier joy nor truer than dreamers may,
Nor more of song than they, nor more of light.

For who sleeps once and sees the secret light
Whereby sleep shows the soul a fairer way

Between the rise and rest of day and night,
Shall care no more to fare as all men may,

But be his place of pain or of delight,
There shall he dwell, beholding night as day.

Song, have thy day and take thy fill of light
Before the night be fallen across thy way;

Sing while he may, man hath no long delight.

16. This poem, by Algernon Charles Swinburne, is a:

a. Sonnet
b. Villanelle
c. Canzonetta
d. Sestina
e. Cavatina

17. Flannery O'Conner's *A Good Man Is Hard To Find* uses situational irony as a plot device. Which of the following plot twists employs this device?

a. Although the grandmother doesn't want to go to Florida with the family, she nonetheless brings along Pitty Sing.
b. The old woman dresses elegantly for the road trip because if she's in an accident, she wants everyone to see her as "a lady."
c. The mother is transformed from a selfish, judgmental liar into a state of redemption by calling the Misfit one of her children.
d. Pitty Sing has her kittens in the basket under the bed.
e. The older mother tells Red Sammy Butts that he is a good man.

18. It is a truth universally acknowledged, that a single man in possession of a good fortune, must be in want of a wife. These are the opening words of:

a. Charlotte Bronte's Jane Eyre
b. Jane Austen's Pride and Prejudice
c. Earnest Hemingway's The Old Man and the Sea
d. Emily Bronte's Wuthering Heights
e. Kate Chopin's The Awakening

Use the following excerpt to answer question 19:

Occupied in observing Mr. Bingley's attentions to her sister, Elizabeth was far from suspecting that she was herself becoming an object of some interest in the eyes of his friend. Mr. Darcy had at first scarcely allowed her to be pretty; he had looked at her without admiration at the ball; and when they next met, he looked at her only to criticise. But no sooner had he made it clear to himself and his friends that she hardly had a good feature in her face, than he began to find it was rendered uncommonly intelligent by the beautiful expression of her dark eyes. To this discovery succeeded some others equally mortifying. Though he had detected with a critical eye more than one failure of perfect symmetry in her form, he was forced to acknowledge her figure to be light and pleasing; and in spite of his asserting that her manners were not those of the fashionable world, he was caught by their easy playfulness. Of this she was perfectly unaware; to her he was only the man who made himself agreeable nowhere, and who had not thought her handsome enough to dance with.

19. The point of view in the above quote, from Jane Austen's *Pride and Prejudice* is:

    a. Omniscient
    b. Third person
    c. First person
    d. Objective
    e. Limited omniscient

20. The *setting* of this novel is an isolated tropical island lacking an exact geographical location. The *time period* is an alternate present. The *characters* are upper class boarding school boys. Interconnected *themes* concern humankind's need for social order, loss of individual identity, and inherent evil in human nature. What novel is this?

    a. Faust
    b. A Farewell to Arms
    c. Brave New World
    d. Lord of the Flies
    e. The Sound and the Fury

21. In what way were Mark Twain's characters similar to those of Kate Chopin?

    a. Both authors created characters based upon family members.
    b. Both authors were more concerned with creating characters that were "types" rather than true to life.
    c. Both authors pushed the envelope of human behavior to the point that their characters became "grotesques."
    d. Both authors were interested in allowing their characters to speak in a way that realistically represented the regional speech of real people.
    e. Both authors created characters that were subtle mockeries of current political figures.

22. Man vs. Man, Man vs. Nature, Man vs. Society, and Man vs. Himself are demonstrated in order in these works:

    a. Les Miserables, The Old Man and the Sea, The Great Gatsby, and Faust
    b. One Hundred Years of Solitude, Moby Dick, Brave New World, and Canterbury Tales
    c. The Last of the Mohicans, The Red Badge of Courage, The Stranger, and A Tale of Two Cities
    d. The Portrait of a Lady, The Woman Warrior, The Magic Mountain, and The Call of the Wild
    e. One Hundred Years of Solitude, The Awakening, Brave New World, and Faust

23. This is an example of _____ and was written by _____.

> The thousand injuries of Fortunato I had borne as best I could, but when he ventured on insult I vowed revenge

a. Motif; Victor Hugo
b. Foreshadowing; Edgar Allen Poe
c. Figurative Language; Theodore Dreiser
d. Hyperbole; Anton Chekhov
e. Paradox; Henry James

24. Lord Alfred Tennyson's famous "murmur of innumerable bees" uses a literary device called:

a. Oxymoron
b. Spondee
c. Synecdoche
d. Onomatopoeia
e. Monotonocheia

25. Catcher in the Rye, To Kill a Mockingbird, Lolita, and One Flew Over the Cuckoo's Nest all share this in common:

a. They were written by Harper Lee.
b. They are representative of early 20th c. works of fiction.
c. They use an unreliable narrator.
d. They are tragic comedies.
e. They were written by women.

Questions 26-28 pertain to the following poem:

Holy Sonnet X

Death, be not proud, though some have called thee
Mighty and dreadful, for thou art not so;
For those whom thou think'st thou dost overthrow,
Die not, poor Death, nor yet canst thou kill me.
From rest and sleep, which but thy pictures be,
Much pleasure; then from thee much more must flow,
And soonest our best men with thee do go,
Rest of their bones, and soul's delivery.
Thou art slave to fate, chance, kings, and desperate men,
And dost with poison, war, and sickness dwell;
And poppy or charms can make us sleep as well
And better than thy stroke; why swell'st thou then?
One short sleep past, we wake eternally,
And death shall be no more; Death, thou shalt die.

26. This poem by John Donne employs:

a. Apostrophe, personification, and paradox
b. Impersonation, metaphor, and triplet
c. Dramatic monologue, tercet, and vagabond
d. Metaphor, personification, and unreliable narration
e. Parody, foil, and hamartia

27. What type of sonnet is this poem?

   a. Shakespearean

   b. Donneian

   c. Petrarchan

   d. Spenserian

   e. Occitan

28. Which lines of this poem contain a pun?

   a. For those whom thou think'st thou dost overthrow

   b. Rest of their bones, and soul's deliver

   c. And soonest our best men with thee do go,

   d. Mighty and dreadful, for thou art not so

   e. And better than thy stroke; why swell'st thou then?

29. Cacophony and euphony refer to:

   a. Chaotic noise and silence in poetry

   b. Unpleasant and pleasant language

   c. Abrupt word endings and sibilant word endings

   d. Melodramatic dialogue and natural dialogue

   e. Allegorical animal speech and human conversation

30. *The Grapes of Wrath* **follows the Joad family, who depend upon a time-honored family structure in which Grandpa is household head and who experience upheaval that turns the traditional sense of family upside down, leaving Ma to lead the family. This familial transformation echoes a societal one, as economic conditions result in more equitable relationships of power among the Weedpatch workers. This is an example of:**

   a. Diatribe

   b. Metaphor

   c. Assonance

   d. Motif

   e. Catharsis

31. This is a story of fratricide, rape, and violence set in the rural south and told from the point of view of a child who writes letters to God and is eventually forced into a loveless marriage that, in spite of all its darkness, is filled with the beauty of an indomitable human spirit. This book was written by:

   a. Eudora Welty

   b. Edith Wharton

   c. Alice Walker

   d. Sylvia Plath

   e. Grace Paley

32. Hyperbole as a literary device stands opposite to:

   a. Synecdoche

   b. Exaggeration

   c. Exclamation

   d. Understatement

   e. Melodrama

33. The Knight, the Pardoner, the Monk, and the Clerk are connected in what way?

a. They appear in the same scene of *One Flew Over the Cuckoo's Nest*.
b. They each appear in a different one of Shakespeare's plays.
c. They are pilgrims.
d. They are off-stage voices in *Waiting for Godot*.
e. There is no relationship between them.

34. Who is the narrator in *Canterbury Tales*?

a. The Host
b. An unnamed, omniscient narrator
c. The narrative role is shared by each character in turn
d. Chaucer
e. An unreliable version of Chaucer

35. How is Love characterized in *Canterbury Tales*?

a. As the Wife of Bath demonstrates, a man's love is temporary, shallow, and never faithful, while the love of a woman reaches beyond the limits of time and space.
b. In the "Knight's Tale," Love is a courtly ideal that needn't be consummated and does not exist within the limits of a marriage.
c. As expressed by the character of Chaucer, Love is an excuse of passionate excess, and being self-indulgent, is therefore impossible to achieve.
d. As the Monk explains, the only true Love is that of a holy man (or, as he grudgingly admits, a woman) for God. Love has no physical or sexual dimension.
e. Love is presented by many of the characters and always to the same end: the idea of Love is mocked and denigrated, denied and used as fodder for jokes.

36. What is the meaning of the coin bank in *Invisible Man*?

a. It symbolizes the importance of "saving" ethnic identity.
b. It is a metaphor for social "change."
c. It has a double meaning: currency (or current social attitudes) and value.
d. It represents stereotypes that are hard to shatter.
e. It symbolizes the importance of investing in an organization (joining with others to defy racism).

37. In *The Turn of the Screw*, which of the following best characterizes James Joyce's use of language?

a. Simple, direct, and unambiguous
b. Convoluted and intentionally both ambiguous and multilayered
c. Complex, circuitous, and embedded
d. Non-linear and experimental
e. None of these; James Joyce is not the author of *The Turn of the Screw*.

38. Which of the following is widely considered to be the first English novel?

a. Robinson Crusoe
b. The Three Musketeers
c. Don Quixote
d. Canterbury Tales
e. Waiting for Godot

39. The five elements of fiction include:

a. Plot, theme, motif, characters, narration
b. Plot, narration, setting, dialogue, action
c. Plot, setting, characters, theme, style
d. Plot, symbols, theme, characters, setting
e. Plot, theme, characters, dialogue, setting

40. This unfinished autobiographical novel takes as its subject the death of the author's father, the importance of faith, and the differences between rural and urban life, and it received a posthumous Pulitzer Prize. The title is:

a. City Mouse, Country Mouse
b. As I Lay Dying
c. Heart of Darkness
d. A Death in the Family
e. An American Tragedy

Questions 41–43 pertain to the following poem:

> They are all gone away,
> The House is shut and still,
> There is nothing more to say.
> Through broken walls and gray
> The winds blow bleak and shrill.
> They are all gone away.
> Nor is there one to-day
> To speak them good or ill:
> There is nothing more to say.
> Why is it then we stray
> Around the sunken sill?
> They are all gone away,
> And our poor fancy-play
> For them is wasted skill:
> There is nothing more to say.
> There is ruin and decay
> In the House on the Hill:
> They are all gone away,
> There is nothing more to say.

41. The title and author of this poem are:

a. Edwin Arlington Robinson, *The House on the Hill*
b. Alexandre Dumas, *There Is Nothing More to Say*
c. Zora Neale Hurston, *In My Father's House*
d. Henrik Ibsen, *A Doll's House*
e. James Joyce, *They Are All Gone Away*

42. This poem is a:

a. Canzone

b. Rondo

c. Chanso

d. Villanelle

e. Ghazal

43. In this poem, "they" refers to:

a. The author's parents

b. The author's ancestors

c. The Gardiners

d. The previous occupants

e. The past

44. What most characterizes the poetry of Robert Frost?

a. Allusion

b. Metaphor

c. Idioms

d. Lyricism

e. Personification

45. Dead, extended, mixed, trope, and synecdoche are related in what way?

a. They are all types of allusions.

b. They are all types of metaphors.

c. They describe stylistic differences.

d. They are different ways of organizing fictional material.

e. These terms have nothing in common.

46. Which of the following are 20th century works?

a. The Bell Jar, Animal Farm, the Catcher in the Rye, Candide, and All Quiet on the Western Front

b. Fathers and Sons, The Adventures of Huckleberry Finn, Slaughterhouse- Five, The Color Purple, and Walden

c. The Bell Jar, Fathers and Sons, Animal Farm, the Catcher in the Rye, and The Picture of Dorian Gray

d. The Bell Jar, Animal Farm, The Catcher in the Rye, All Quiet on the Western Front, and As I Lay Dying

e. Slaughterhouse- Five, The Color Purple, The Catcher in the Rye, War and Peace, and Vanity Fair

47. What do *The Color Purple* and *The Awakening* have in common?

a. Both books are 20th century novellas.

b. Both books were written by social reformers.

c. Both books were banned for sexual content.

d. Both books were banned for social commentary.

e. Both books were originally written under aliases.

48. Is ambiguity a useful device for a writer?

a. Yes. Ambiguity allows a text to be interpreted in multiple ways.
b. No. An ambiguous text is too difficult to understand.
c. Yes. An ambiguous text is "larger than life" and encompasses many motifs and themes.
d. No. An ambiguous text offers confusing or even contradictory meanings.
e. A and D.

49. Why is the novel *Ulysses* one of the most important 20th c. works of fiction?

a. B, C, D, and E.
b. It is one of the most important works of the Modernist movement.
c. It is highly experimental in nature.
d. It reinvents the epic poem *Ulysses* for contemporary readers.
e. It is filled with historic and literary allusions and unexpected word play that makes readers conscious of the material of language.

50. What genre is One Hundred Years of Solitude?

a. Contemporary realism
b. Epistolary
c. Magical realism
d. Episodic
e. Melodramatic fiction

Questions 51 – 56 pertain to the following passage:

Percy Bysshe Shelley, "Ozymandias"

I met a traveller from an antique land
Who said: "Two vast and trunkless legs of stone
Stand in the desert. Near them on the sand,
Half sunk, a shattered visage lies, whose frown
And wrinkled lip and sneer of cold command
Tell that its sculptor well those passions read
Which yet survive, stamped on these lifeless things,
The hand that mocked them and the heart that fed.
And on the pedestal these words appear:
`My name is Ozymandias, King of Kings:
Look on my works, ye mighty, and despair!'
Nothing beside remains. Round the decay
Of that colossal wreck, boundless and bare,
The lone and level sands stretch far away."

51. What is the rhyme scheme of the first eight lines?

a. ABACADAC
b. ABABACDC
c. ABABABCB
d. ABADACDC
e. ABABCBCB

52. What is the central image of the poem?

a. A collapsed statue in the desert
b. A wounded king
c. A face and inscription on a coin
d. A plaque near a WWII battle site
e. The Sphinx

53. In what sense are lines 10-11 ironic? Although the inscription was originally intended to boast of a king's power, it appears to later generations as an example of how:

a. Engineering skills were not as advanced as people believed at the time
b. A king's power extends only as far as the boundaries of his kingdom
c. A king can attain immortality through his works
d. Time and nature will eventually undo the works of even the mighty
e. The desert is not a suitable climate for a kingdom

54. Read as a symbol, the desert can be seen to represent:

a. Fertility
b. The life cycle
c. The seasons
d. Life
e. A wasteland

55. Based on the setting, which of the following do you think best describes Ozymandias?

a. Roman Emperor
b. Egyptian Pharaoh
c. Native American Chief
d. Dynastic Emperor
e. English Monarch

56. What poetic form does this poem use?

a. Italian sonnet
b. Ballad
c. Anaphora
d. Prose poem
e. Sestina

Questions 57 – 60 pertain to the following passage:

Emily Dickinson, "Success is counted sweetest"

Success is counted sweetest
By those who ne'er succeed.
To comprehend a nectar
Requires sorest need.

Not one of all the purple Host
Who took the Flag today
Can tell the definition
So clear of Victory

As he defeated--dying--
On whose forbidden ear
The distant strains of triumph
Burst agonized and clear!

57. In the final stanza, the imagery suggests a soldier who lies dying on a battlefield. Which of the following interpretations of lines from the poem reinforce this image?

I. The final line suggests cannon blasts
II. "Strains of triumph" imply the dying soldier's joy in victory
III. The words "defeated, dying" in line 9 indicate mortal combat

a. I only
b. I and II
c. II and III
d. I and III
e. II only

58. What literary device is employed in lines 3 and 4?

a. Paradox
b. Caesura
c. Metaphor
d. Dramatic monologue
e. Anaphora

59. How many stressed syllables are in each line of the first stanza?

a. 1
b. 2
c. 3
d. 4
e. 5

60. By what logical pattern is this poem organized?

a. Main idea, developed with examples
b. Cause and effect
c. Comparison and contrast
d. Chronological order
e. Description

Answers and Explanations 2

1. D: When an author uses dramatic irony, he is making a clear division between the written work and the world of the reader. Dramatic irony offers the reader enough information in the form of hints, dramatic action, or exposition, to be able to clearly understand something obvious that a character, usually through a character flaw, is absolutely unable to see. Sophocles' Oedipus Rex uses dramatic irony, both when he murders his own father on the road, failing to recognize him as anything other than a traveler, and then when he marries a woman whom the reader realizes is his own mother.

2. E: Flannery O'Conner, classified as a Southern writer along with William Faulkner and Eudora Welty, is best known for her peculiar, even grotesque characters. Her stories inevitably end in violence and death, and her characters are typically odd in appearance, action, or both. O'Conner, a devout Catholic, seems at first glance to be uncompassionate and cruel. A more careful reading finds that these freakish characters are representative of the fractured human existence that results from the fall from grace.

3. E: Iambic pentameter is the most common rhythmic pattern in English poetry, as well as in informal conversation. An iamb is a rhythmic "foot" and contains two "steps," or beats. Pentameter, of course, means five. Iambic pentameter is a five-foot line in poetry that contains a total of ten "steps;" the stress is placed on the second beat of each set. While in theory iambic pentameter is very regular, in practice poets may use literary license to occasionally stress the first syllable of a word in order to draw attention to the image or concept contained in the line.

4. C: Shakespeare's poem is in praise of the beauty of youth. By comparing to young man to elements in nature—a summer's day, rough winds, delicate buds—he finds the youth's beauty will be eternal, whereas beauty in nature is temporal.

5. D: "When in eternal lines to time thou growest" can mean a few different things, depending upon how the meaning is assigned to "lines." Seen as lineage, the youth's beauty will be passed from generation to generation, remaining alive and untouched "as long as men can live." "Lines" can also be read as lines of poetry; in this, Shakespeare is making (possibly ironic) reference to his own "eternal lines" that will live as long as "eyes can see."

6. B: Dante Alighieri's *The Divine Comedy* is organized into three canticas: Inferno, Purgatorio, and Paradiso. The lines are tercets rhyming aba, bcb, cdc, etc. The work covers a fictional period during which time a first-person narrator (whom most consider to be Dante himself) visits the Inferno and the Purgatorio with Virgil and Heaven with his adored Beatrice. *The Divine Comedy* has continued to maintain a reputation as one of the finest pieces of writing from any culture, and it is of central importance to Italian literature. Dante intended a complexity of meanings. *The Divine Comedy* can be read as an historical document; a moral treatise; a literal representation of the afterlife; or an anagoge, by which a reader can ascend to greater spiritual heights. Adding to the complexity are the mathematical and magical patterns of threes (a reference to the Trinity) and nines.

7. C: In Toni Morrison's prize-winning novel *Beloved*, Sethe is absolutely dedicated to her children. She has gone through so much personal trauma—of the body, the heart, and the spirit—that she cannot imagine inflicting it upon them. As slaves, however, it is inevitable. She cannot accept at first that Beloved is, in fact, her own beloved, murdered child, and when she does, Beloved herself enslaves her mother with guilt until Sethe is able to find her balance, take hold of both the past and the present, and insist upon a life that is truly free.

110

8. C: In *Mrs. Dalloway*, Woolf explores narrative use of time through a shifting, highly intimate third-person point of view that passes from character to character. The novel begins early on the day during which Clarissa Dalloway and her husband, Richard, will host a party. It continues throughout the hours of the day and early evening, and then concludes deep in the night. Although the novel's real time is a single day, the reader discovers past events, the memories of which are triggered by events or sensory stimuli within that single day. One of the things that holds the novel together is the sense of uneasy dissatisfaction the characters all embody. While each had grand intentions for their lives, ultimately, each has arrived at the realization, or at least an undercurrent of sense, that those earlier expectations will never be met. When Septimus, a war veteran, leaps to his death to avoid being institutionalized, Clarissa feels that, somehow, she has caused it.

9. B: The ongoing debate regarding the origins of the early Anglo-Saxon epic poem *Beowulf* has largely settled into two camps. The first gained popularity midway through the second half of the last century, hypothesizing the poem is the written artifact of oral Grendel tales passed down from generation to generation, embroidered as each teller saw fit until a scribe collected the various related tales and codified them into a single work rich with tribal, heroic, Germanic, and pagan influences. The opposition position holds that it is the composition of one individual, who, being literate, knowing Latin, and most likely a monk, wrote the text from a Christian viewpoint.

10. C: This essay is the Spring section from Walden. Thoreau built a small cabin Walden Pond in 1845 where he lived and wrote in relative isolation. Walden, published in 1854, celebrates the simple life, the ultimate morality of nature, and independence. The book is simultaneously poetic, single-minded, richly detailed, scientifically sound and deeply philosophical.

11. E: Thoreau is saying that Nature doesn't give up, no matter how massive the obstacles she faces are. Storms produce new life and new shorelines; new life forms spring up within a decaying, fallen tree. By recognizing the determination of the life-force, we will be "refreshed" and able to understand that whatever limits we experience have been placed there by ourselves. When we witness "some life pasturing freely where we never wander," it can inspire and embolden us to transcend our limits.

12. C: Universal innocence is Thoreau's answer to the Garden of Eden. His "garden," however, is not blissful, perfect, or kind. It is a place where death occurs in order to give birth to life, or simply because "Nature is so rife with life that myriads can be…sacrificed…" He does not see this as evidence of an unkind or wasteful God, but as an ultimately soothing and even forgiving event. Wounds are not fatal (even when they end a life, because life continues), and poison is not poison. All who participate in the continuity of life are universally innocent.

13. B: William Carlos Williams, a physician and important member of the early 20th c. Imagist movement, called for a new kind of poetry that stripped off the ornaments of Romantic and Victorian writing in favor of simple, vivid images within which meaning resided. Both Eliot and Pound filled their work with literary references that required educated readers. Williams, although highly educated, wanted poetry to simply serve truth through honest, pure image. The Imagist movement began the period of Modern poetry, and Williams' influence is profound. He mentored Charles Olsen (founder of the Black Mountain school, which included Robert Creeley, Denise Levertov, and some of the Beat poets); associated with Kenneth Rexroth, founder of the San Francisco Renaissance; and influenced Gary Snyder, Philip Whalen, and Allen Ginsberg.

14. A: *Gulliver's Travels*, Jonathan Swift's 1726 novel, satirizes human nature while it poses as a travel book. Gulliver, who was "first a surgeon, then a captain of several ships," visits several obscure countries whose inhabitants symbolize various aspects of human nature. The Lilliputians,

tiny as a thumb, believe their little lives are hugely important. In order to survive among the Brogdingnagians, to whom he is a toy, Gulliver must pay microscopic attention to the minutiae of the physical, and sometimes private, world, a world largely ignored by his times; the Brobdingnagians symbolize the physical realm. The Laputans are symbolic of theory that has no practical application, has never been tested, and has never been proven. During the Enlightenment, new theories were common; Swift shows himself as a conservative here. Houyhnhnms symbolize the Platonic Ideal in their love of reason, their honesty, and their moderation in all things.

15. E: Abigail, who is worried she will be punished for her wild dancing and casting of charms in the woods, realizes that a false confession in which she claims, essentially, that the Devil made her do it will resolve her from guilt and offer her redemption. In the process, she names a number of others as witches in order to deflect further attention. When her friends see that she is successful, they join her in calling out other women as witches, which rapidly devolves into the mass hysteria that resulted in many deaths.

16. E: This is a sestina. The first six stanzas contain six lines each and repeat the same six end words in a mathematically determined progression as follows: (1) A.B.C.D.E.F., (2) F.A.E.B.D.C., (3) C.F.D.A.B.E., (4) E.C.B.F.A.D., (5) D.E.A.C.F.B., (6) B.D.F.E.C.A. The seventh stanza is an envoy composed of three lines; words B and A appear in the first line; D and C in the second; and F and E in the third. A troubadour, Arnaut Daniel, created the form in the 12th c., and it was later adapted and popularized by Francesco Petrarca.

17. C: Situational irony operates by leading the reader away from an expected outcome through a plot twist to an unexpected realization. In *A Good Man Is Hard To Find*, the mother is manipulative, selfish, and racist. She tells lies and places her own desires above others. She causes the accident that attracts the Misfit, then blurts out his identity rather than behaving as though she doesn't recognize him. While the Misfit's cohorts are murdering her family in the woods, the mother recognizes that the Misfit contains as much good as evil, and that she, ironically, contains as much darkness as goodness. In that moment, when reaching out to him with forgiveness, she is transformed just before he shoots her.

18. B: When Mrs. Bennet speaks these words to Mr. Bennet, she is thinking of her own five daughters and their financially precarious situation. Their estate is owned by a relative who will reclaim it should Mr. Bennet die, leaving the women of the family unprotected. A wealthy husband would ensure the future of all five daughters. Mr. Bingly, a new, wealthy, and single neighbor, is the subject of Mrs. Bennet's musings. Bingly is likeable and friendly; his friend, Darcy, is cool and standoffish; and Bingly's sisters, who are staying with him, are critically judgmental of Mrs. Bennet's rough manners. The 18th century novel's emphasis on a rich variety of strictly-controlled social relationships concerned with caste and class is reflective of the of the time period.

19. E: A limited omniscient narrator is able to see inside the mind of a single character, knows that character's feelings and thoughts, and perceives all action as it pertains to that single character. An omniscient narrator is able to visit the minds of any character at any point in time; this novelistic position gives the greatest sense of narrative reliability. In contrast, a story told from the first person, or "I" point of view, in which the story is told solely through the voice and experiences of a single character who narrates, is the least reliable form of narration and the most dramatic. A story told from the objective point of view reports action and records dialogue, but the minds and feelings of characters remain closed to the reader.

20. D: William Golding's *The Lord of the Flies* follows upper-class boys ages five to twelve as they create and then destroy their own society after their plane crashes on an island following their

evacuation from England in the midst of an atomic war. They fend for themselves, first under Ralph's leadership, who advocates order and reason but is susceptible to passion. Jack, Ralph's jealous nemesis, a demonic, violent leader, rules by fear. Both Simon, the Christ- figure, and Piggy, the intellectual, are killed by the others, all of whom fear the invisible Beastie, a symbol of the evil within human nature.

21. D: The Chopin novel *The Awakening*, set on Grand Isles and New Orleans in the French Quarter at the turn of the century, accurately captures the cadence and colloquialisms of the Creole and French influences on both the English language and on the culture. Mark Twain's stories are primarily set along the Mississippi River, and his characters' dialogue is richly laced with the idioms and pace of the people and the times.

22. A: In general, most literary theorists agree that the conflict in all literary works of art can be organized into seven categories. In addition to Man vs. Man, Man vs. Nature, Man vs. Society, and Man vs. Himself can be added the categories of Man vs. Machine, exemplified by Mary Shelley's *Frankenstein*; Man vs. God, as found in the *Odyssey* or Hermann Hesse's *Siddhartha*; and Man vs. the Supernatural, for example, Edgar Allen Poe's *The Tell- Tale Heart*.

23. B: Edgar Allen Poe is a master of foreshadowing, a literary device in which the author plants clues that suggest a pivotal event that will take place at some later point in the story. Foreshadowing can take form as a single sentence, a piece of dialogue, even a description of the weather, or it can involve a fully fleshed out scene that portends things to come.

24. D: Onomatopoeia is not only a fun word to say, it is also a widely used literary device in which the words themselves suggest, by their sounds, that which they are describing. It comes from the Greek word for "name," coupled with "I make." Onomatopoeia is frequently used in poetry, but it is also commonly (though more subtly) used in fiction. Animal names, such as chickadee or cuckoo, can be onomatopoetic, and frequently words that represent sounds do so by imitating them: *crunch, giggle, howl,* and *drip* are examples.

25. C: These novels all employ an unreliable, or fallible, first-person narrator. Unreliable narrators are used by authors to offer an intentionally defective filter through which other characters and story action are offered. The reader, being fully aware that the narrator has a "hidden" agenda, lacks the knowledge or wisdom to correctly interpret story action, is a pathological liar, suffers from a mental or emotional disorder, or in some other way cannot be trusted to establish and relay objective truth, must read between the lines. By forcing the reader to interpret the story, the author is drawing the reader deeply into the fictional fabric, involving her almost to the point of becoming part of the story.

26. A: The dramatic opening lines of *Holy Sonnet X* speak directly to Death. Such a direct address to someone or something that isn't physically or literally present and cannot respond is called apostrophe. By speaking to Death as though it were a living, present being, John Donne is employing personification. Personification treats inanimate objects, concepts, or non-human creatures as though they were human, as a metaphoric device. A paradox appears on the surface to contain contradictory ideas, and for this reason requires a reader to closely examine the language to find deeper meanings that resolve the contradiction. *Holy Sonnet X* paradoxically announces that Death itself will die, a statement that at first reading is absurd. The deeper meaning, that life continues beyond death, resolves the paradox.

27. C: While there are many types of sonnets, most literary theorists group them into English and Italian forms. All sonnets contain 14 lines and are generally written in iambic pentameter. The

Italian, or Petrarchan, sonnet is composed of an eight-line stanza called an octave, followed by a six-line stanza, or sestet. Traditionally, the octave follows an abbaabba rhyme scheme, while the sestet has a number of rhyme options. The English, or Shakespearean, sonnet, divides its 14 lines into three four-line stanzas, or quatrains, followed by a rhyming couplet. The quatrains are most often rhymed abab, cdcd, efef, and the couplet, gg. A Spenserian sonnet is just a variation of English sonnet, and an Occitan sonnet is one written in Medieval French.

28. E: Donne frequently included sexual innuendos and puns in his religious poems. Shocking as it may seem now, his clever use of language to suggest multiple meanings was reflective of his time. For example, "die" once carried the meaning of sexual climax in addition to the meaning we know today. Given Donne's belief that life continues despite death and beyond it, and given that sexuality is the means by which life continues itself on earth, the pun is both understandable and brilliant. "Stroke" simultaneously becomes the stroke of death and the stroke of sexual penetration, as both the sexual organ and Death's own ego are inflated.

29. B: Cacophony, or language that is unpleasant, loud, jarring, jangling, abrupt, or otherwise unpleasant, is often used intentionally and to great effect by an author. An abundance of consonants, single-syllable words, and words containing harsh blends create cacophony. The most famous examples are found in Lewis Carroll's *The Jabberwocky*. In contrast, euphonious language is intentionally manipulated to create soothing, melodious language. The opening line of John Keats' *To Autumn* contains an exquisite example that invites the reader to enter the poem through the sweetness of its sounds: "Season of mists and mellow fruitfulness."

30. D: Motifs are found in nearly all works of art, and they are one of the ways in which a work simultaneously organizes and enriches itself. A motif is a recurring pattern, structure, or relationship that offers both decorative detail and contributes to meaning. Motifs can manifest as an object that reappears through the course of the work; a place that characters return to; a phrase or statement that is repeated by one character, more than one character, or the narrator; or a type of story action. Motifs are symbolic of ideas; in this Steinbeck novel, *The Grapes of Wrath*, the recurring motif of the necessary disintegration of traditional social structures that don't serve equitably is seen in the Joads and in the workers at the camp.

31. C: *The Color Purple*, Pulitzer Prize-winning author Alice Walker's most famous work, has been censored, banned, and celebrated. The plot is complex, even convoluted, involving dozens of characters whose relationships extend over many years and cover continents. In addition to novels, Walker's poems and short fiction address the same themes. Her work is concerned with problems of violence—especially violence to women and children, racism, dysfunctional families and relationships, and how different generations see the same reality. Despite these dark themes, her writing brims with beauty, seeks healing, and expresses deep joy.

32. D: Hyperbole in poetry, fiction, or nonfiction is an intentional exaggeration, often to ridiculous proportions, for effect. The intention may be to underscore or emphasize a point the author or a character is attempting to make, to mock or ridicule a character or situation within the writing or within the culture that the writing reflects, or simply to entertain or amuse. Because children take such delight in hyperbole, tall tales are rich with it, as exemplified by Paul Bunyan stories. Mark Twain is a master of hyperbole, as is Flannery O'Connor, particularly when she describes characters: "The skin on her face was as thin and drawn as tight as the skin of onion and her eyes were gray and sharp like the points of two picks." ("Parker's Back").

33. C: These characters from Chaucer's *Canterbury Tales* join the Squire, the Knight's Yeoman, The Prioress, Hubert, The Merchant, The Man of Law, and many others as they make a pilgrimage to

114

visit Thomas Becket's shrine. The pilgrims gather at the Tabard Inn, and each is assigned to tell two stories as they travel to the destination and two returning home. The stories are told with much hilarity, insult, interruption, and drama. With each tale, the social structure and relationships between characters becomes more complex and interwoven, as each character represents an occupation or a type, rather than a unique, distinct individual.

34. E: Although the narrator presents himself as both Chaucer and a character on the pilgrimage, he provides enough evidence to make it clear that he is neither a reliable reflection of Chaucer, the man, nor is he a reliable narrator. While he describes himself as friendly and unsophisticated, other characters, most notably the Host, find him surly. Although his role is Narrator, he doesn't write down the stories until later, remembering both the tellers and the tales as he prefers to, which simultaneously makes his version suspect and paints a more vivid portrait of the character of the Narrator than of any other character.

35. B: Courtly love was central to much of the literary arts of the Middle Ages, celebrated as an ideal that was as much a spiritual desire as a physical one. Love brings a man to his knees, making him desire only to serve his lady. Love is primarily a male activity, and a man in love embraces its all-devouring temperament. In addition, love is capable of causing a lover tremendous hardship, pain, and suffering.

36. D: The coin bank, which looks like a wide-mouthed black man who grovels for a few coins, is a stereotype that persists even after the bank has been shattered by the narrator. Throughout the novel, a number of characters bring the broken bits of the coin bank to the narrator, wrapped in paper.

37. E: The author of *The Turn of the Screw, Daisy Miller, Portrait of a Lady*, and other short stories and novels is Henry James. His writing style is elaborate, layered, and richly embroidered, with many complex sentences composed of numerous embedded clauses that cast a backwards illumination on clauses that appeared earlier in the sentence, sometimes a number of lines before.

38. A: Daniel Defoe's oddly-titled, "Strange Surprizing Adventures of Robinson Crusoe of York, Mariner: Who lived Eight and Twenty Years, all alone in an un-inhabited Island on the coast of America, near the Mouth of the Great River of Oroonoque; Having been cast on Shore by Shipwreck, where-in all the Men perished but himself. With An Account how he was at last as strangely deliver'd by Pyrates. Written by Himself," quickly took the alternate title, *Robinson Crusoe*. It appeared in 1719 and is presented as a fictionalized autobiography of a castaway rescued only after 36 years. Although Defoe's geographic island is similar to Tobago, the story itself was inspired by an actual castaway who lived for four years on an island off the Chilean coast.

39. C: Plot is story action and the reasons behind it. Setting involves the locations where the story unfolds. Characters are, of course, the people or animated objects in the story that interact and communicate. The story's theme is the single most important idea, around which all other elements of the story are organized. A theme, which is abstract, is not the same as a topic, but it is manifested through story action, characters, motifs, and so forth. Authorial style includes the highly conscious selection and arrangement of words to express the story's ideas and is a matter of art in that multiple meaning, language sound and rhythms, narrative position, the story's tone, the structural relationship of all elements, and other subtle manipulations all contribute to style.

40. D: James Agee's *A Death in the Family* explores the author's memories following the accidental death of his father, as well as the tension in the nation's growth toward urban centers and away from rural life. Because Agee, an alcoholic and smoker, died of a heart attack before the manuscript

was complete, it was left to his editors to decide which of several versions to publish. Interestingly, they chose to italicize the incomplete portions and publish them at the conclusion of the appropriate section already created by Agee. It is very likely that the book Agee intended to write would have been much longer, and possibly not as linearly sequential as the one that did appear, composed of twenty chapters.

41. A: Edwin Arlington Robinson did not intend this poem to represent any actual house and took offense at writer Amy Lowell's claim that it was inspired by the local Oaklands estate. Robinson's life was far from happy. His own parents didn't give him a name for the first six months of his life, and they then allowed a name to be selected from a hat at a vacation resort. A drug overdose was responsible for his brother's death, and his brother's widow spurned Robinson's repeated proposals of marriage. After his father's death, he grew more and more impoverished, self publishing a first, unsuccessful book and later a second one that resulted in a White House appointment at the NY Customs Office. His career was finally established when he won the Pulitzer Prize three times.

42. D: *The House on the Hill* is a villanelle. A villanelle is a six-stanza poem, each of which in composed of three lines except the final stanza, which contains four. In each stanza there is a repeating line that alternates; stanzas 1, 3, and 5 share a repeating line, as do stanzas 2, 4, and 6. The final stanza contains both repeating lines. In addition to the fixed form and repeating lines, villanelles offer an aba rhyme scheme. The poetic form offers a special challenge in that the simple, circular rhyme scheme and reappearance of the same two lines throughout the poem require the poet to move slowly through the material. Dylan Thomas's *Do Not Go Gentle Into That Good Night* and Elizabeth Bishop's *One Art* are two of the best-known examples of villanelles in English.

43. E: By Edwin Arlington Robinson's own admission, *The House on the Hill* is a fabrication and does not refer to any structure that has ever stood, although poet Amy Lowell assumed it was connected to a mansion once owned by the Gardiner family. The best reading of the poem is that it is not only everyone who has occupied the past that has gone away, but it is also the past itself. There is no use is trying to conjure it; *there is nothing left to say*, and one's interpretation is likewise useless, *To speak them good or ill*; although people cannot help but refer to the past in terms that celebrate or denigrate it. Yet, people continue to *stray/Around the sunken sill* looking for meaning in what once stood, because inevitably we will all belong to the past.

44. B: Metaphor is often defined as a direct comparison between two unlike things. While many poets create metaphors by borrowing attributes from one object and assigning them to another as a way to express an idea or emotion. Shakespeare's Jacque, in *As You Like It*, declares that *All the world's a stage/and all the men and women merely players.* For Robert Frost, the essence of poetry was in finding the profound within the trivial. Frost's *The Road Not Taken* uses the metaphor of a road leading into a future the writer (and the reader) can never experience as a metaphor for choice and commitment.

45. B: Dead metaphors are those that have abandoned their metaphoric value in favor of an understood, idiomatic one, such as "happy as a clam." An extended metaphor compares two things by assigning a characteristic found in one to the other and continues to allusion over the length of a poem, essay, short story, or novel. A mixed metaphor, which incorrectly combines images or characteristics from unrelated sources, is the result of carelessness or inexperience on the part of the writer. An example of this is "The starry-eyed lovers sailed off into the sunset." A trope is any type of figurative language. Synecdoche is a figure of speech in which something is metaphorically represented by part of that thing; for example, "many moons ago" meanings many months ago.

46. D: *The Bell Jar* by Sylvia Plath was published in 1963; George Orwell's *Animal Farm* appeared in 1945; *The Catcher in the Rye*, written by J.D. Salinger, made its first appearance in 1951; *All Quiet on the Western Front*, a novel about World War I, (called the Great War), was written by Erich Maria Remarque and published in 1929; and William Faulkner's *As I Lay Dying* appeared in 1930. These novels accurately reflect the social changes of their times or consider a relatively newly self-conscious psychological landscape.

47. C: Kate Chopin's 1898 novel *The Awakening* is set in French Creole Louisiana. It was attacked by critics soon after it appeared, and it was banned by the Evanston Public Library in 1902 for its sexually-suggestive content. Given the straitlaced Victorian attitudes of the day, Chopin was extremely subtle with her language; however, Edna Pontellier's sexual liaison with Alcee Arubin did not escape detection. Alice Walker's *The Color Purple* appeared nearly a full century later, but it, too, was highly criticized and banned at a number of public institutions, ostensibly for sexual content, which included the rape of a child, sexual liaisons outside marriage, and a lesbian affair. Regardless of the controversy that initially surrounded it, the novel went on to win a Pulitzer Prize.

48. E: Ambiguity can, in fact, either deeply enrich a text, offering a multiplicity of possible meanings or multiple meanings that enhance one another, or it can be deeply confusing. Whether ambiguity is successful or not depends upon the writer's controlled intentions. Literary ambiguity that enhances a text is never an accident. For an event, a theme, an idea, or even an understanding of a character to be interpreted a number of ways without causing confusion, the author must be very aware of every possible interpretation and must weave them together and tease them apart, both deliberately and at controlled intervals.

49. A: There is no doubt that James Joyce's *Ulysses* is one of, if not the most, influential works of fiction of the 20th century. First published in 1922, it is a stunning opus of literary allusion, humor, and meditations on the human experience. It includes every type of language play imaginable, including puns, wildly extended metaphors, intoxicatingly poetic language and seductive rhythms, and richly-realized characterizations. Ultimately, it shows a self-reflective awareness of itself as a novel, with the reader as a participant in the act of reading and language as music, as meaning, as meaningless, and as paint. Although the substantial novel contains nearly 300,000 words, many phrases repeat, invert, echo, and imitate themselves; in all, this vast work is composed of a total vocabulary of only 30,000.

50. C: Gabriel Garcia Marquez' *One Hundred Years of Solitude* is the quintessential representative of magical realism. It spans generations that are both drenched in supernatural events and that mirror the political turmoil of the times. Novels that can be assigned to the category of magical realism treat the unearthly aspects as everyday occurrences; moments of supernatural imposition are neither dwelled upon nor minimized. Magical realism is a highly literary genre, much more sophisticated than either science fiction or fantasy in that the elements of otherworldliness are treated as ordinary, coexist with a "normal" reality, and are noted by the narrator and sometimes—but not always—by the characters. As well, works of magical realism typically show a passion for the linguistic surface and metaphor.

51. B: The rhyme scheme of the first eight lines falls into the following pattern: ABABACDC. The rhyming words are, "land," "stone," "sand," "frown," "command," "read," "things," and "fed."

52. A: A collapsed statue in the desert. The image is explicitly described in lines 2 through 4: "Two vast and trunkless legs of stone / Stand in the desert. Near them on the sand, / Half sunk, a shattered visage lies." None of the other choices reflect the imagery of the poem.

53. D: Is the best interpretation of the ironic meaning of the inscription. Irony is used to describe statements or events with multiple levels of meaning. Specifically, it is defined as a statement in which the apparent meaning of the words contradicts the intended meaning. In this case, the poem describes a collapsed statue with an inscription that reads, "Look upon my works, ye mighty, and despair." The original intended meaning of the words was that one should look upon the majesty of Ozymandias's kingdom and despair because of his power. When read underneath a ruined statue, however, the words take on a different apparent meaning, namely that the reader should look at the kingdom and despair because of the destructive forces of time and nature.

54: E: The symbolic meaning of the desert is best read as a wasteland. A symbol is a specific image in a poem that brings to mind some idea or concept that relates back to the poem's themes. Choice (A), fertility, is not likely since a desert rarely calls fertility to mind. Choice (B), the life cycle, is likewise not commonly associated with the desert. Choice (C), the seasons, does not relate to the poem in any meaningful way. Choice (D), life, is so broad that it could be applied to any symbol and does not yield much insight into the themes of this particular poem. Choice (E), a wasteland, is a connotation (or associated meaning) of the desert that does relate back to the theme of the poem, which has to do with the destructive forces of time and the comparative powerlessness of humans.

55. B: An Egyptian Pharaoh, is the best answer because of the poem's setting among ruins in the desert. Choice (A), a Roman Emperor, may be suggested by collapsed statues, but not by the desert landscape. The desert landscape would not refer to choices (C), (D), or (E)—leaders of Native American, Chinese, or English cultures.

56. A: The poem has fourteen lines, which makes the poem a sonnet. Choice (B), ballad, refers to a type of poem with four-line stanzas and iambic meter. Choice (C), anaphora, is a way of creating emphasis by repeating words at the beginning of each line. Choice (D), prose poem, is a more recent form of poetry that does not have line breaks and resembles paragraphs of prose. Choice (E), sestina, refers to a poem with six-line stanzas in which each line ends with one of the same six words.

57. D: The question provides you with an interpretation of the poem. Your job is to identify any of the following statements that help support or prove that interpretation. Choice (D), interpretations I and III, is the best choice. Interpretation II suggests that the dying soldier was victorious in battle, but line nine, "as he defeated, dying" contradicts this reading. Interpretations I and II both reinforce the reading of the stanza as a scene from a battle.

58: C: A metaphor is an implied comparison between two things. In the first stanza, Dickinson creates an implicit comparison between success and nectar (the sweet fluid produced by plants); since she does not use "like" or "as," this type of comparison is called a metaphor, as opposed to a simile, which does. Choice (A), paradox, which means the poem contains contradictory ideas, may be true of the poem as a whole, but metaphor is the best choice for the specific lines three and four because of the implied comparison Dickinson draws between success and nectar. Choice (B), caesura, refers to a pause within the line, but these lines read without pause. Choice (D), dramatic monologue, is a poetic form written in first person in which the speaker is a character in the poem; however, the speaker of Dickinson's poem does not act as a character in the poem. Choice (E), anaphora, is a rhetorical device using repetition, and this poem does not rely heavily on repetition.

59. C: 3 beats per line, is the best answer. With the syllables stressed, the first stanza reads:

> SucCESS is COUNted SWEEtest
> By THOSE who NE'ER sucCEED.
> To COMPreHEND a NECTar
> ReQUIres SORest NEED.

Note that there are three stressed syllables per line. The poem varies this structure in the second stanza, adding a fourth stressed syllable in the first line, but for the most part, Dickinson's poem is written in iambic trimeter. "Iambic" refers to a pattern of syllables in which every other syllable is stressed. "Trimeter" means there are three beats per line.

60. A: Dickinson states the main argument of the poem in the first line and provides examples in the form of metaphors to develop that idea. Choice (B), cause and effect, is not the main logical organization of the poem, as this method usually involves isolating a main cause and explaining the effects that result from it. Choice (C), comparison and contrast, most often involves pointing out the similarities and differences between two things, which this poem does not do at length. Choice (D), chronological order, involves describing an event from its first to last moments. Dickinson's poem focuses on multiple events and does not tell which happened first or last. Choice (E), description, usually examines the details of a single item or event; this poem, however, does not provide a great deal of detail for detail's sake.

How to Overcome Test Anxiety

Just the thought of taking a test is enough to make most people a little nervous. A test is an important event that can have a long-term impact on your future, so it's important to take it seriously and it's natural to feel anxious about performing well. But just because anxiety is normal, that doesn't mean that it's helpful in test taking, or that you should simply accept it as part of your life. Anxiety can have a variety of effects. These effects can be mild, like making you feel slightly nervous, or severe, like blocking your ability to focus or remember even a simple detail.

If you experience test anxiety—whether severe or mild—it's important to know how to beat it. To discover this, first you need to understand what causes test anxiety.

Causes of Test Anxiety

While we often think of anxiety as an uncontrollable emotional state, it can actually be caused by simple, practical things. One of the most common causes of test anxiety is that a person does not feel adequately prepared for their test. This feeling can be the result of many different issues such as poor study habits or lack of organization, but the most common culprit is time management. Starting to study too late, failing to organize your study time to cover all of the material, or being distracted while you study will mean that you're not well prepared for the test. This may lead to cramming the night before, which will cause you to be physically and mentally exhausted for the test. Poor time management also contributes to feelings of stress, fear, and hopelessness as you realize you are not well prepared but don't know what to do about it.

Other times, test anxiety is not related to your preparation for the test but comes from unresolved fear. This may be a past failure on a test, or poor performance on tests in general. It may come from comparing yourself to others who seem to be performing better or from the stress of living up to expectations. Anxiety may be driven by fears of the future—how failure on this test would affect your educational and career goals. These fears are often completely irrational, but they can still negatively impact your test performance.

> **Review Video: 3 Reasons You Have Test Anxiety**
> Visit mometrix.com/academy and enter code: 428468

120

Elements of Test Anxiety

As mentioned earlier, test anxiety is considered to be an emotional state, but it has physical and mental components as well. Sometimes you may not even realize that you are suffering from test anxiety until you notice the physical symptoms. These can include trembling hands, rapid heartbeat, sweating, nausea, and tense muscles. Extreme anxiety may lead to fainting or vomiting. Obviously, any of these symptoms can have a negative impact on testing. It is important to recognize them as soon as they begin to occur so that you can address the problem before it damages your performance.

Review Video: 3 Ways to Tell You Have Test Anxiety
Visit mometrix.com/academy and enter code: 927847

The mental components of test anxiety include trouble focusing and inability to remember learned information. During a test, your mind is on high alert, which can help you recall information and stay focused for an extended period of time. However, anxiety interferes with your mind's natural processes, causing you to blank out, even on the questions you know well. The strain of testing during anxiety makes it difficult to stay focused, especially on a test that may take several hours. Extreme anxiety can take a huge mental toll, making it difficult not only to recall test information but even to understand the test questions or pull your thoughts together.

Review Video: How Test Anxiety Affects Memory
Visit mometrix.com/academy and enter code: 609003

Effects of Test Anxiety

Test anxiety is like a disease—if left untreated, it will get progressively worse. Anxiety leads to poor performance, and this reinforces the feelings of fear and failure, which in turn lead to poor performances on subsequent tests. It can grow from a mild nervousness to a crippling condition. If allowed to progress, test anxiety can have a big impact on your schooling, and consequently on your future.

Test anxiety can spread to other parts of your life. Anxiety on tests can become anxiety in any stressful situation, and blanking on a test can turn into panicking in a job situation. But fortunately, you don't have to let anxiety rule your testing and determine your grades. There are a number of relatively simple steps you can take to move past anxiety and function normally on a test and in the rest of life.

Review Video: How Test Anxiety Impacts Your Grades
Visit mometrix.com/academy and enter code: 939819

Physical Steps for Beating Test Anxiety

While test anxiety is a serious problem, the good news is that it can be overcome. It doesn't have to control your ability to think and remember information. While it may take time, you can begin taking steps today to beat anxiety.

Just as your first hint that you may be struggling with anxiety comes from the physical symptoms, the first step to treating it is also physical. Rest is crucial for having a clear, strong mind. If you are tired, it is much easier to give in to anxiety. But if you establish good sleep habits, your body and mind will be ready to perform optimally, without the strain of exhaustion. Additionally, sleeping well helps you to retain information better, so you're more likely to recall the answers when you see the test questions.

Getting good sleep means more than going to bed on time. It's important to allow your brain time to relax. Take study breaks from time to time so it doesn't get overworked, and don't study right before bed. Take time to rest your mind before trying to rest your body, or you may find it difficult to fall asleep.

Review Video: The Importance of Sleep for Your Brain
Visit mometrix.com/academy and enter code: 319338

Along with sleep, other aspects of physical health are important in preparing for a test. Good nutrition is vital for good brain function. Sugary foods and drinks may give a burst of energy but this burst is followed by a crash, both physically and emotionally. Instead, fuel your body with protein and vitamin-rich foods.

Also, drink plenty of water. Dehydration can lead to headaches and exhaustion, especially if your brain is already under stress from the rigors of the test. Particularly if your test is a long one, drink water during the breaks. And if possible, take an energy-boosting snack to eat between sections.

Review Video: How Diet Can Affect your Mood
Visit mometrix.com/academy and enter code: 624317

Along with sleep and diet, a third important part of physical health is exercise. Maintaining a steady workout schedule is helpful, but even taking 5-minute study breaks to walk can help get your blood pumping faster and clear your head. Exercise also releases endorphins, which contribute to a positive feeling and can help combat test anxiety.

When you nurture your physical health, you are also contributing to your mental health. If your body is healthy, your mind is much more likely to be healthy as well. So take time to rest, nourish your body with healthy food and water, and get moving as much as possible. Taking these physical steps will make you stronger and more able to take the mental steps necessary to overcome test anxiety.

Review Video: How to Stay Healthy and Prevent Test Anxiety
Visit mometrix.com/academy and enter code: 877894

Mental Steps for Beating Test Anxiety

Working on the mental side of test anxiety can be more challenging, but as with the physical side, there are clear steps you can take to overcome it. As mentioned earlier, test anxiety often stems from lack of preparation, so the obvious solution is to prepare for the test. Effective studying may be the most important weapon you have for beating test anxiety, but you can and should employ several other mental tools to combat fear.

First, boost your confidence by reminding yourself of past success—tests or projects that you aced. If you're putting as much effort into preparing for this test as you did for those, there's no reason you should expect to fail here. Work hard to prepare; then trust your preparation.

Second, surround yourself with encouraging people. It can be helpful to find a study group, but be sure that the people you're around will encourage a positive attitude. If you spend time with others who are anxious or cynical, this will only contribute to your own anxiety. Look for others who are motivated to study hard from a desire to succeed, not from a fear of failure.

Third, reward yourself. A test is physically and mentally tiring, even without anxiety, and it can be helpful to have something to look forward to. Plan an activity following the test, regardless of the outcome, such as going to a movie or getting ice cream.

When you are taking the test, if you find yourself beginning to feel anxious, remind yourself that you know the material. Visualize successfully completing the test. Then take a few deep, relaxing breaths and return to it. Work through the questions carefully but with confidence, knowing that you are capable of succeeding.

Developing a healthy mental approach to test taking will also aid in other areas of life. Test anxiety affects more than just the actual test—it can be damaging to your mental health and even contribute to depression. It's important to beat test anxiety before it becomes a problem for more than testing.

Review Video: Test Anxiety and Depression
Visit mometrix.com/academy and enter code: 904704

Study Strategy

Being prepared for the test is necessary to combat anxiety, but what does being prepared look like? You may study for hours on end and still not feel prepared. What you need is a strategy for test prep. The next few pages outline our recommended steps to help you plan out and conquer the challenge of preparation.

STEP 1: SCOPE OUT THE TEST

Learn everything you can about the format (multiple choice, essay, etc.) and what will be on the test. Gather any study materials, course outlines, or sample exams that may be available. Not only will this help you to prepare, but knowing what to expect can help to alleviate test anxiety.

STEP 2: MAP OUT THE MATERIAL

Look through the textbook or study guide and make note of how many chapters or sections it has. Then divide these over the time you have. For example, if a book has 15 chapters and you have five days to study, you need to cover three chapters each day. Even better, if you have the time, leave an extra day at the end for overall review after you have gone through the material in depth.

If time is limited, you may need to prioritize the material. Look through it and make note of which sections you think you already have a good grasp on, and which need review. While you are studying, skim quickly through the familiar sections and take more time on the challenging parts. Write out your plan so you don't get lost as you go. Having a written plan also helps you feel more in control of the study, so anxiety is less likely to arise from feeling overwhelmed at the amount to cover. A sample plan may look like this:

- Day 1: Skim chapters 1–4, study chapter 5 (especially pages 31–33)
- Day 2: Study chapters 6–7, skim chapters 8–9
- Day 3: Skim chapter 10, study chapters 11–12 (especially pages 87–90)
- Day 4: Study chapters 13–15
- Day 5: Overall review (focus most on chapters 5, 6, and 12), take practice test

STEP 3: GATHER YOUR TOOLS

Decide what study method works best for you. Do you prefer to highlight in the book as you study and then go back over the highlighted portions? Or do you type out notes of the important information? Or is it helpful to make flashcards that you can carry with you? Assemble the pens, index cards, highlighters, post-it notes, and any other materials you may need so you won't be distracted by getting up to find things while you study.

If you're having a hard time retaining the information or organizing your notes, experiment with different methods. For example, try color-coding by subject with colored pens, highlighters, or post-it notes. If you learn better by hearing, try recording yourself reading your notes so you can listen while in the car, working out, or simply sitting at your desk. Ask a friend to quiz you from your flashcards, or try teaching someone the material to solidify it in your mind.

STEP 4: CREATE YOUR ENVIRONMENT

It's important to avoid distractions while you study. This includes both the obvious distractions like visitors and the subtle distractions like an uncomfortable chair (or a too-comfortable couch that makes you want to fall asleep). Set up the best study environment possible: good lighting and a comfortable work area. If background music helps you focus, you may want to turn it on, but otherwise keep the room quiet. If you are using a computer to take notes, be sure you don't have any other windows open, especially applications like social media, games, or anything else that could distract you. Silence your phone and turn off notifications. Be sure to keep water close by so you stay hydrated while you study (but avoid unhealthy drinks and snacks).

Also, take into account the best time of day to study. Are you freshest first thing in the morning? Try to set aside some time then to work through the material. Is your mind clearer in the afternoon or evening? Schedule your study session then. Another method is to study at the same time of day that you will take the test, so that your brain gets used to working on the material at that time and will be ready to focus at test time.

STEP 5: STUDY!

Once you have done all the study preparation, it's time to settle into the actual studying. Sit down, take a few moments to settle your mind so you can focus, and begin to follow your study plan. Don't give in to distractions or let yourself procrastinate. This is your time to prepare so you'll be ready to fearlessly approach the test. Make the most of the time and stay focused.

Of course, you don't want to burn out. If you study too long you may find that you're not retaining the information very well. Take regular study breaks. For example, taking five minutes out of every hour to walk briskly, breathing deeply and swinging your arms, can help your mind stay fresh.

As you get to the end of each chapter or section, it's a good idea to do a quick review. Remind yourself of what you learned and work on any difficult parts. When you feel that you've mastered the material, move on to the next part. At the end of your study session, briefly skim through your notes again.

But while review is helpful, cramming last minute is NOT. If at all possible, work ahead so that you won't need to fit all your study into the last day. Cramming overloads your brain with more information than it can process and retain, and your tired mind may struggle to recall even previously learned information when it is overwhelmed with last-minute study. Also, the urgent nature of cramming and the stress placed on your brain contribute to anxiety. You'll be more likely to go to the test feeling unprepared and having trouble thinking clearly.

So don't cram, and don't stay up late before the test, even just to review your notes at a leisurely pace. Your brain needs rest more than it needs to go over the information again. In fact, plan to finish your studies by noon or early afternoon the day before the test. Give your brain the rest of the day to relax or focus on other things, and get a good night's sleep. Then you will be fresh for the test and better able to recall what you've studied.

STEP 6: TAKE A PRACTICE TEST

Many courses offer sample tests, either online or in the study materials. This is an excellent resource to check whether you have mastered the material, as well as to prepare for the test format and environment.

Check the test format ahead of time: the number of questions, the type (multiple choice, free response, etc.), and the time limit. Then create a plan for working through them. For example, if you have 30 minutes to take a 60-question test, your limit is 30 seconds per question. Spend less time on the questions you know well so that you can take more time on the difficult ones.

If you have time to take several practice tests, take the first one open book, with no time limit. Work through the questions at your own pace and make sure you fully understand them. Gradually work up to taking a test under test conditions: sit at a desk with all study materials put away and set a timer. Pace yourself to make sure you finish the test with time to spare and go back to check your answers if you have time.

After each test, check your answers. On the questions you missed, be sure you understand why you missed them. Did you misread the question (tests can use tricky wording)? Did you forget the information? Or was it something you hadn't learned? Go back and study any shaky areas that the practice tests reveal.

Taking these tests not only helps with your grade, but also aids in combating test anxiety. If you're already used to the test conditions, you're less likely to worry about it, and working through tests until you're scoring well gives you a confidence boost. Go through the practice tests until you feel comfortable, and then you can go into the test knowing that you're ready for it.

Test Tips

On test day, you should be confident, knowing that you've prepared well and are ready to answer the questions. But aside from preparation, there are several test day strategies you can employ to maximize your performance.

First, as stated before, get a good night's sleep the night before the test (and for several nights before that, if possible). Go into the test with a fresh, alert mind rather than staying up late to study.

Try not to change too much about your normal routine on the day of the test. It's important to eat a nutritious breakfast, but if you normally don't eat breakfast at all, consider eating just a protein bar. If you're a coffee drinker, go ahead and have your normal coffee. Just make sure you time it so that the caffeine doesn't wear off right in the middle of your test. Avoid sugary beverages, and drink enough water to stay hydrated but not so much that you need a restroom break 10 minutes into the test. If your test isn't first thing in the morning, consider going for a walk or doing a light workout before the test to get your blood flowing.

Allow yourself enough time to get ready, and leave for the test with plenty of time to spare so you won't have the anxiety of scrambling to arrive in time. Another reason to be early is to select a good seat. It's helpful to sit away from doors and windows, which can be distracting. Find a good seat, get out your supplies, and settle your mind before the test begins.

When the test begins, start by going over the instructions carefully, even if you already know what to expect. Make sure you avoid any careless mistakes by following the directions.

Then begin working through the questions, pacing yourself as you've practiced. If you're not sure on an answer, don't spend too much time on it, and don't let it shake your confidence. Either skip it and come back later, or eliminate as many wrong answers as possible and guess among the remaining ones. Don't dwell on these questions as you continue—put them out of your mind and focus on what lies ahead.

Be sure to read all of the answer choices, even if you're sure the first one is the right answer. Sometimes you'll find a better one if you keep reading. But don't second-guess yourself if you do immediately know the answer. Your gut instinct is usually right. Don't let test anxiety rob you of the information you know.

If you have time at the end of the test (and if the test format allows), go back and review your answers. Be cautious about changing any, since your first instinct tends to be correct, but make sure

you didn't misread any of the questions or accidentally mark the wrong answer choice. Look over any you skipped and make an educated guess.

At the end, leave the test feeling confident. You've done your best, so don't waste time worrying about your performance or wishing you could change anything. Instead, celebrate the successful completion of this test. And finally, use this test to learn how to deal with anxiety even better next time.

> **Review Video: 5 Tips to Beat Test Anxiety**
> Visit mometrix.com/academy and enter code: 570656

Important Qualification

Not all anxiety is created equal. If your test anxiety is causing major issues in your life beyond the classroom or testing center, or if you are experiencing troubling physical symptoms related to your anxiety, it may be a sign of a serious physiological or psychological condition. If this sounds like your situation, we strongly encourage you to seek professional help.

How to Overcome Your Fear of Math

The word *math* is enough to strike fear into most hearts. How many of us have memories of sitting through confusing lectures, wrestling over mind-numbing homework, or taking tests that still seem incomprehensible even after hours of study? Years after graduation, many still shudder at these memories.

The fact is, math is not just a classroom subject. It has real-world implications that you face every day, whether you realize it or not. This may be balancing your monthly budget, deciding how many supplies to buy for a project, or simply splitting a meal check with friends. The idea of daily confrontations with math can be so paralyzing that some develop a condition known as *math anxiety*.

But you do NOT need to be paralyzed by this anxiety! In fact, while you may have thought all your life that you're not good at math, or that your brain isn't wired to understand it, the truth is that you may have been conditioned to think this way. From your earliest school days, the way you were taught affected the way you viewed different subjects. And the way math has been taught has changed.

Several decades ago, there was a shift in American math classrooms. The focus changed from traditional problem-solving to a conceptual view of topics, de-emphasizing the importance of learning the basics and building on them. The solid foundation necessary for math progression and confidence was undermined. Math became more of a vague concept than a concrete idea. Today, it is common to think of math, not as a straightforward system, but as a mysterious, complicated method that can't be fully understood unless you're a genius.

This is why you may still have nightmares about being called on to answer a difficult problem in front of the class. Math anxiety is a very real, though unnecessary, fear.

Math anxiety may begin with a single class period. Let's say you missed a day in 6th grade math and never quite understood the concept that was taught while you were gone. Since math is cumulative, with each new concept building on past ones, this could very well affect the rest of your math career. Without that one day's knowledge, it will be difficult to understand any other concepts that link to it. Rather than realizing that you're just missing one key piece, you may begin to believe that you're simply not capable of understanding math.

This belief can change the way you approach other classes, career options, and everyday life experiences, if you become anxious at the thought that math might be required. A student who loves science may choose a different path of study upon realizing that multiple math classes will be required for a degree. An aspiring medical student may hesitate at the thought of going through the necessary math classes. For some this anxiety escalates into a more extreme state known as *math phobia*.

Math anxiety is challenging to address because it is rooted deeply and may come from a variety of causes: an embarrassing moment in class, a teacher who did not explain concepts well and contributed to a shaky foundation, or a failed test that contributed to the belief of math failure.

These causes add up over time, encouraged by society's popular view that math is hard and unpleasant. Eventually a person comes to firmly believe that he or she is simply bad at math. This belief makes it difficult to grasp new concepts or even remember old ones. Homework and test grades begin to slip, which only confirms the belief. The poor performance is not due to lack of ability but is caused by math anxiety.

Math anxiety is an emotional issue, not a lack of intelligence. But when it becomes deeply rooted, it can become more than just an emotional problem. Physical symptoms appear. Blood pressure may rise and heartbeat may quicken at the sight of a math problem – or even the thought of math! This fear leads to a mental block. When someone with math anxiety is asked to perform a calculation, even a basic problem can seem overwhelming and impossible. The emotional and physical response to the thought of math prevents the brain from working through it logically.

The more this happens, the more a person's confidence drops, and the more math anxiety is generated. This vicious cycle must be broken!

The first step in breaking the cycle is to go back to very beginning and make sure you really understand the basics of how math works and why it works. It is not enough to memorize rules for multiplication and division. If you don't know WHY these rules work, your foundation will be shaky and you will be at risk of developing a phobia. Understanding mathematical concepts not only promotes confidence and security, but allows you to build on this understanding for new concepts. Additionally, you can solve unfamiliar problems using familiar concepts and processes.

Why is it that students in other countries regularly outperform American students in math? The answer likely boils down to a couple of things: the foundation of mathematical conceptual understanding and societal perception. While students in the US are not expected to *like* or *get* math, in many other nations, students are expected not only to understand math but also to excel at it.

Changing the American view of math that leads to math anxiety is a monumental task. It requires changing the training of teachers nationwide, from kindergarten through high school, so that they learn to teach the *why* behind math and to combat the wrong math views that students may develop. It also involves changing the stigma associated with math, so that it is no longer viewed as unpleasant and incomprehensible. While these are necessary changes, they are challenging and will take time. But in the meantime, math anxiety is not irreversible—it can be faced and defeated, one person at a time.

False Beliefs

One reason math anxiety has taken such hold is that several false beliefs have been created and shared until they became widely accepted. Some of these unhelpful beliefs include the following:

There is only one way to solve a math problem. In the same way that you can choose from different driving routes and still arrive at the same house, you can solve a math problem using different methods and still find the correct answer. A person who understands the reasoning behind math calculations may be able to look at an unfamiliar concept and find the right answer, just by applying logic to the knowledge they already have. This approach may be different than what is taught in the classroom, but it is still valid. Unfortunately, even many teachers view math as a subject where the best course of action is to memorize the rule or process for each problem rather than as a place for students to exercise logic and creativity in finding a solution.

Many people don't have a mind for math. A person who has struggled due to poor teaching or math anxiety may falsely believe that he or she doesn't have the mental capacity to grasp mathematical concepts. Most of the time, this is false. Many people find that when they are relieved of their math anxiety, they have more than enough brainpower to understand math.

Men are naturally better at math than women. Even though research has shown this to be false, many young women still avoid math careers and classes because of their belief that their math abilities are inferior. Many girls have come to believe that math is a male skill and have given up trying to understand or enjoy it.

Counting aids are bad. Something like counting on your fingers or drawing out a problem to visualize it may be frowned on as childish or a crutch, but these devices can help you get a tangible understanding of a problem or a concept.

Sadly, many students buy into these ideologies at an early age. A young girl who enjoys math class may be conditioned to think that she doesn't actually have the brain for it because math is for boys, and may turn her energies to other pursuits, permanently closing the door on a wide range of opportunities. A child who finds the right answer but doesn't follow the teacher's method may believe that he is doing it wrong and isn't good at math. A student who never had a problem with math before may have a poor teacher and become confused, yet believe that the problem is because she doesn't have a mathematical mind.

Students who have bought into these erroneous beliefs quickly begin to add their own anxieties, adapting them to their own personal situations:

I'll never use this in real life. A huge number of people wrongly believe that math is irrelevant outside the classroom. By adopting this mindset, they are handicapping themselves for a life in a mathematical world, as well as limiting their career choices. When they are inevitably faced with real-world math, they are conditioning themselves to respond with anxiety.

I'm not quick enough. While timed tests and quizzes, or even simply comparing yourself with other students in the class, can lead to this belief, speed is not an indicator of skill level. A person can work very slowly yet understand at a deep level.

If I can understand it, it's too easy. People with a low view of their own abilities tend to think that if they are able to grasp a concept, it must be simple. They cannot accept the idea that they are capable of understanding math. This belief will make it harder to learn, no matter how intelligent they are.

I just can't learn this. An overwhelming number of people think this, from young children to adults, and much of the time it is simply not true. But this mindset can turn into a self-fulfilling prophecy that keeps you from exercising and growing your math ability.

The good news is, each of these myths can be debunked. For most people, they are based on emotion and psychology, NOT on actual ability! It will take time, effort, and the desire to change, but change is possible. Even if you have spent years thinking that you don't have the capability to understand math, it is not too late to uncover your true ability and find relief from the anxiety that surrounds math.

Math Strategies

It is important to have a plan of attack to combat math anxiety. There are many useful strategies for pinpointing the fears or myths and eradicating them:

Go back to the basics. For most people, math anxiety stems from a poor foundation. You may think that you have a complete understanding of addition and subtraction, or even decimals and percentages, but make absolutely sure. Learning math is different from learning other subjects. For example, when you learn history, you study various time periods and places and events. It may be important to memorize dates or find out about the lives of famous people. When you move from US history to world history, there will be some overlap, but a large amount of the information will be new. Mathematical concepts, on the other hand, are very closely linked and highly dependent on each other. It's like climbing a ladder – if a rung is missing from your understanding, it may be difficult or impossible for you to climb any higher, no matter how hard you try. So go back and make sure your math foundation is strong. This may mean taking a remedial math course, going to a tutor to work through the shaky concepts, or just going through your old homework to make sure you really understand it.

Speak the language. Math has a large vocabulary of terms and phrases unique to working problems. Sometimes these are completely new terms, and sometimes they are common words, but are used differently in a math setting. If you can't speak the language, it will be very difficult to get a thorough understanding of the concepts. It's common for students to think that they don't understand math when they simply don't understand the vocabulary. The good news is that this is fairly easy to fix. Brushing up on any terms you aren't quite sure of can help bring the rest of the concepts into focus.

Check your anxiety level. When you think about math, do you feel nervous or uncomfortable? Do you struggle with feelings of inadequacy, even on concepts that you know you've already learned? It's important to understand your specific math anxieties, and what triggers them. When you catch yourself falling back on a false belief, mentally replace it with the truth. Don't let yourself believe that you can't learn, or that struggling with a concept means you'll never understand it. Instead, remind yourself of how much you've already learned and dwell on that past success. Visualize grasping the new concept, linking it to your old knowledge, and moving on to the next challenge. Also, learn how to manage anxiety when it arises. There are many techniques for coping with the irrational fears that rise to the surface when you enter the math classroom. This may include controlled breathing, replacing negative thoughts with positive ones, or visualizing success. Anxiety interferes with your ability to concentrate and absorb information, which in turn contributes to greater anxiety. If you can learn how to regain control of your thinking, you will be better able to pay attention, make progress, and succeed!

Don't go it alone. Like any deeply ingrained belief, math anxiety is not easy to eradicate. And there is no need for you to wrestle through it on your own. It will take time, and many people find that speaking with a counselor or psychiatrist helps. They can help you develop strategies for responding to anxiety and overcoming old ideas. Additionally, it can be very helpful to take a short course or seek out a math tutor to help you find and fix the missing rungs on your ladder and make sure that you're ready to progress to the next level. You can also find a number of math aids online: courses that will teach you mental devices for figuring out problems, how to get the most out of your math classes, etc.

Check your math attitude. No matter how much you want to learn and overcome your anxiety, you'll have trouble if you still have a negative attitude toward math. If you think it's too hard, or just have general feelings of dread about math, it will be hard to learn and to break through the anxiety. Work on cultivating a positive math attitude. Remind yourself that math is not just a hurdle to be cleared, but a valuable asset. When you view math with a positive attitude, you'll be much more likely to understand and even enjoy it. This is something you must do for yourself. You may find it helpful to visit with a counselor. Your tutor, friends, and family may cheer you on in your endeavors. But your greatest asset is yourself. You are inside your own mind – tell yourself what you need to hear. Relive past victories. Remind yourself that you are capable of understanding math. Root out any false beliefs that linger and replace them with positive truths. Even if it doesn't feel true at first, it will begin to affect your thinking and pave the way for a positive, anxiety-free mindset.

Aside from these general strategies, there are a number of specific practical things you can do to begin your journey toward overcoming math anxiety. Something as simple as learning a new note-taking strategy can change the way you approach math and give you more confidence and understanding. New study techniques can also make a huge difference.

Math anxiety leads to bad habits. If it causes you to be afraid of answering a question in class, you may gravitate toward the back row. You may be embarrassed to ask for help. And you may procrastinate on assignments, which leads to rushing through them at the last moment when it's too late to get a better understanding. It's important to identify your negative behaviors and replace them with positive ones:

Prepare ahead of time. Read the lesson before you go to class. Being exposed to the topics that will be covered in class ahead of time, even if you don't understand them perfectly, is extremely helpful in increasing what you retain from the lecture. Do your homework and, if you're still shaky, go over some extra problems. The key to a solid understanding of math is practice.

Sit front and center. When you can easily see and hear, you'll understand more, and you'll avoid the distractions of other students if no one is in front of you. Plus, you're more likely to be sitting with students who are positive and engaged, rather than others with math anxiety. Let their positive math attitude rub off on you.

Ask questions in class and out. If you don't understand something, just ask. If you need a more in-depth explanation, the teacher may need to work with you outside of class, but often it's a simple concept you don't quite understand, and a single question may clear it up. If you wait, you may not be able to follow the rest of the day's lesson. For extra help, most professors have office hours outside of class when you can go over concepts one-on-one to clear up any uncertainties. Additionally, there may be a *math lab* or study session you can attend for homework help. Take advantage of this.

Review. Even if you feel that you've fully mastered a concept, review it periodically to reinforce it. Going over an old lesson has several benefits: solidifying your understanding, giving you a confidence boost, and even giving some new insights into material that you're currently learning! Don't let yourself get rusty. That can lead to problems with learning later concepts.

Teaching Tips

While the math student's mindset is the most crucial to overcoming math anxiety, it is also important for others to adjust their math attitudes. Teachers and parents have an enormous influence on how students relate to math. They can either contribute to math confidence or math anxiety.

As a parent or teacher, it is very important to convey a positive math attitude. Retelling horror stories of your own bad experience with math will contribute to a new generation of math anxiety. Even if you don't share your experiences, others will be able to sense your fears and may begin to believe them.

Even a careless comment can have a big impact, so watch for phrases like *He's not good at math* or *I never liked math*. You are a crucial role model, and your children or students will unconsciously adopt your mindset. Give them a positive example to follow. Rather than teaching them to fear the math world before they even know it, teach them about all its potential and excitement.

Work to present math as an integral, beautiful, and understandable part of life. Encourage creativity in solving problems. Watch for false beliefs and dispel them. Cross the lines between subjects: integrate history, English, and music with math. Show students how math is used every day, and how the entire world is based on mathematical principles, from the pull of gravity to the shape of seashells. Instead of letting students see math as a necessary evil, direct them to view it as an imaginative, beautiful art form – an art form that they are capable of mastering and using.

Don't give too narrow a view of math. It is more than just numbers. Yes, working problems and learning formulas is a large part of classroom math. But don't let the teaching stop there. Teach students about the everyday implications of math. Show them how nature works according to the laws of mathematics, and take them outside to make discoveries of their own. Expose them to math-related careers by inviting visiting speakers, asking students to do research and presentations, and learning students' interests and aptitudes on a personal level.

Demonstrate the importance of math. Many people see math as nothing more than a required stepping stone to their degree, a nuisance with no real usefulness. Teach students that algebra is used every day in managing their bank accounts, in following recipes, and in scheduling the day's events. Show them how learning to do geometric proofs helps them to develop logical thinking, an invaluable life skill. Let them see that math surrounds them and is integrally linked to their daily lives: that weather predictions are based on math, that math was used to design cars and other machines, etc. Most of all, give them the tools to use math to enrich their lives.

Make math as tangible as possible. Use visual aids and objects that can be touched. It is much easier to grasp a concept when you can hold it in your hands and manipulate it, rather than just listening to the lecture. Encourage math outside of the classroom. The real world is full of measuring, counting, and calculating, so let students participate in this. Keep your eyes open for numbers and patterns to discuss. Talk about how scores are calculated in sports games and how far apart plants are placed in a garden row for maximum growth. Build the mindset that math is a normal and interesting part of daily life.

Finally, find math resources that help to build a positive math attitude. There are a number of books that show math as fascinating and exciting while teaching important concepts, for example: *The Math Curse; A Wrinkle in Time; The Phantom Tollbooth;* and *Fractals, Googols and Other Mathematical Tales.* You can also find a number of online resources: math puzzles and games, videos that show math in nature, and communities of math enthusiasts. On a local level, students can compete in a variety of math competitions with other schools or join a math club.

The student who experiences math as exciting and interesting is unlikely to suffer from math anxiety. Going through life without this handicap is an immense advantage and opens many doors that others have closed through their fear.

Self-Check

Whether you suffer from math anxiety or not, chances are that you have been exposed to some of the false beliefs mentioned above. Now is the time to check yourself for any errors you may have accepted. Do you think you're not wired for math? Or that you don't need to understand it since you're not planning on a math career? Do you think math is just too difficult for the average person?

Find the errors you've taken to heart and replace them with positive thinking. Are you capable of learning math? Yes! Can you control your anxiety? Yes! These errors will resurface from time to time, so be watchful. Don't let others with math anxiety influence you or sway your confidence. If you're having trouble with a concept, find help. Don't let it discourage you!

Create a plan of attack for defeating math anxiety and sharpening your skills. Do some research and decide if it would help you to take a class, get a tutor, or find some online resources to fine-tune your knowledge. Make the effort to get good nutrition, hydration, and sleep so that you are operating at full capacity. Remind yourself daily that you are skilled and that anxiety does not control you. Your mind is capable of so much more than you know. Give it the tools it needs to grow and thrive.

Thank You

We at Mometrix would like to extend our heartfelt thanks to you, our friend and patron, for allowing us to play a part in your journey. It is a privilege to serve people from all walks of life who are unified in their commitment to building the best future they can for themselves.

The preparation you devote to these important testing milestones may be the most valuable educational opportunity you have for making a real difference in your life. We encourage you to put your heart into it—that feeling of succeeding, overcoming, and yes, conquering will be well worth the hours you've invested.

We want to hear your story, your struggles and your successes, and if you see any opportunities for us to improve our materials so we can help others even more effectively in the future, please share that with us as well. **The team at Mometrix would be absolutely thrilled to hear from you!** So please, send us an email (support@mometrix.com) and let's stay in touch.

> **If you'd like some additional help, check out these other resources we offer for your exam:**
> http://mometrixflashcards.com/SATII

Additional Bonus Material

Due to our efforts to try to keep this book to a manageable length, we've created a link that will give you access to all of your additional bonus material.

Please visit http://www.mometrix.com/bonus948/satliterature to access the information.

11908196R00083

Made in the USA
Monee, IL
19 September 2019